STATE AND LAW IN EASTERN ASIA

To remember Edward Shils
Teacher, guide, and friend

State and Law in Eastern Asia

Edited by

LESLIE PALMIER
Asian Studies Centre
St Antony's College
Oxford, UK

Dartmouth

Aldershot • Brookfield USA • Singapore • Sydney

Published by
Dartmouth Publishing Company Limited
Gower House
Croft Road
Aldershot
Hants GU11 3HR
England

Dartmouth Publishing Company
Old Post Road
Brookfield
Vermont 05036
USA

British Library Cataloguing in Publication Data
State and law in Eastern Asia
   1.Rule of law - East Asia 2.Rule of law - Asia, Southeastern
   3.East Asia - Constitutional law 4.Asia, Southeastern - Constitutional law
   I.Palmier, Leslie H. (Leslie Hugh), 1924-
   340.1'1'095

Library of Congress Cataloging-in-Publication Data
State and law in eastern Asia / edited by Leslie Palmier.
     p.   cm.
   Papers presented at a seminar series at the Asian Studies Centre,
St. Antony's College, Oxford, Oct.-Nov. 1993.
   Includes bibliographical references.
   ISBN 1-85521-781-3 (H)
   1. Rule of law–East Asia. I. Palmier, Leslie H.
KNC514.S73   1996
340'.11–dc20   96-21350
                                   CIP

ISBN 1 85521 781 3

Printed and bound by Athenaeum Press, Ltd.,
Gateshead, Tyne & Wear.

Contents

Contents

Contributors

Philip Baker is a barrister, member of Gray's Inn Chambers, and a frequent visitor to China, with a long-standing interest in Chinese law, and primary interest in human rights. From 1979 to 1985 he was lecturer in law (specialising in Chinese law) at the School of Oriental and African Studies, London University; since then, he has been visiting lecturer and is now visiting fellow at the school.

Hiroshi Oda held the chair of Soviet Law at the University of Tokyo before, in 1990, being appointed Sir Ernest Satow Professor of Japanese Law at University College, London. He continues to advise the Japanese ministries of Justice and of International Trade and Industry.

Adnan Buyung Nasution, the most prominent human rights activist in Indonesia, practices law in Jakarta. He was founder and is honorary director of the Indonesian Legal Aid Institute.

Andrew Harding is senior lecturer in law at the School of Oriental and African Studies, University of London, and was formerly senior lecturer in the Law Faculty, National University of Singapore.

Vitit Muntarbhorn is professor of international law at Chulalongkorn University, Bangkok, and barrister of the Middle Temple. He is also United Nations Special Rapporteur on the Sale of Children, and Executive Director of Child Rights ASIANET.

Leslie Palmier was reader in sociology at the University of Bath and associate fellow at St Antony's College, Oxford. He has long had a special concern with Asia, particularly Indonesia.

Preface

These papers, first presented at a seminar series at the Asian Studies Centre at St Antony's College, Oxford, in October and November 1993, embody its best traditions. They are scholarly and timely contributions to an issue of major global and regional concern, they allow us to examine that issue from a comparative perspective, and they include voices from the region as well as outside. Authors touch on the core issue of state legality, and demonstrate that it is a matter of concern and debate within these Asian societies, not just in the West.

The Centre would like to thank the authors and, especially, Dr Leslie Palmier who convened the seminar series and has edited this collection, for allowing a wider audience to benefit from their informed views on this important topic.

Rosemary Foot
Director
Asian Studies Centre
St Antony's College, Oxford

Introduction

LESLIE PALMIER

The contributors to this volume consider China, Indonesia, Japan, Singapore, and Thailand with regard to rule of law. It is important to distinguish this from 'law and order', with which it is often confused. The one does not imply the latter. Rule of law refers specifically to the state itself being accountable under the laws to an independent authority, usually the judiciary. Rule of law should also be clearly distinguished from *l'état de droit* of French jurisprudence, which refers to 'a state which considers the law as itself premised upon a number of higher imperatives which are of an ethical nature'.[1] Rule of law has no such moral ambitions.

A state may not be subject to rule of law, but enforce its laws with great vigour, as do many tyrannies; and rule of law may prevent a state from oppressing its citizens, who nevertheless frequently break laws. With this distinction in mind, we may now proceed to consider the very different legal histories of the five states which are the subject of this symposium.

In China, only at the end of the 19th century was any attempt made to write modernized legal codes. In spite of half a dozen parliamentary constitutions drawn up between 1912 and 1928, the country degenerated into virtual anarchy, with the nominal government at Peking subject to warlords who ruled large parts of the country. The Kuomintang in 1928 established a central government of five branches, one of them judicial. But all their officials were members of the Kuomintang party, and they were supervised by its Central Executive Committee. There was no hint of judicial independence from the executive. In 1936 a draft of constitutional government was published, but in practice there was 'a rigorous punitive censorship of the press, a large network of secret police and prisons, and a massive "white terror" flourishing in the cities and towns ...'.[2] In 1937 matters were made worse by the outbreak of war with Japan. Her defeat by the allies in 1945 ushered in a four-year war between the Kuomintang and the Communist Party, ending in complete victory for the latter in 1949; they reinforced the police state. The present-day situation is discussed in the next chapter by Philip Baker.

In the Netherlands Indies, as Indonesia then was, only at the beginning of last century were the first steps taken to introduce rule of law. In a report of 1803 directed at remedying abuses of administration bequeathed by the bankrupt East India Company, the principle was enunciated that there should be a careful distinction between judiciary and executive, so as to prevent arbitrary interference with the course of justice. The report also argued for a new Supreme Court, the members of which would all be appointed from Europe. These principles were adopted and extended by Daendels, Governor-General between 1808 and 1811. In practice, he did not hesitate to expel the President of the High Court of Justice for showing signs of independence.[3]

Codification of Dutch law after 1815 led to its revision. In accordance with the principle of indirect rule adopted by the Dutch, 'Europeans were placed under the law, and Natives left to the executive'. The local indigenous governors, known as regents, were given precedence over the prosecuting Judge Advocate. This dual organization of society was reasserted in the Constitutional Regulation of 1854, which provided for the independence of the judiciary, but left Indonesians under their 'appointed or recognized heads'. In future law was to take the place of arbitrary rule; but this principle came into effect very slowly. The regents were not closely bound by law until early in the next century, while what the Dutch termed 'gentle pressure', the exercise of personal authority beyond the law, continued until the end of their rule. The press still had only limited freedom, and no political assembly was permitted.[4]

Rule of law was inched further in 1910 when the magisterial power of Native officials was restricted to legally defined offences. At the same time, the duality of judicial administration began to erode. In 1914 a police court was constituted with jurisdiction over all classes of the community; the same applied to a penal code introduced four years later. This process did not go far. Criminal matters came before European Courts if the parties were Europeans, and before Native Courts if they were Indonesians or 'Foreign Orientals' (mainly Chinese). Similarly, civil law for Europeans and 'Foreign Orientals' was much the same as in the Netherlands; that for Indonesians was based on their customary law, which had absorbed some elements of Islamic jurisprudence. (However, the benches of the High Court and the six Courts of Justice administering European law might include Indonesians, while the President in a Native Court might be a European.)[5]

Furthermore, judicial administration discriminated strongly between Europeans and Indonesians. Legally trained judges sat in the European courts, but in the Native courts two of the four members were active or retired indigenous officials. Most importantly, perhaps, Indonesians, though not Europeans, could be held in jail under 'preventive detention' without judicial authority.[6] These powers were used liberally to repress political dissent, particularly in the 1930s. It would be difficult to argue that Indonesians had experienced rule of law.

This of course does not mean that 'law and order' was lacking. On the contrary, so strongly was it enforced, particularly by informal measures, that capital punishment had practically been abolished; the sentences imposed in the Native Courts were (by comparison with Burma under British rule) 'ridiculously lenient'; no suggestion was ever heard of corruption in the courts, and the police had little work, as crimes were so rare.[7]

The Japanese occupation and subsequent Indonesian independence ended all duality. On the other hand, as Adnan

Buyung Nasution shows in a later chapter, rule of law has been abandoned, and courts are firmly under control by the executive.

Japan saw the beginnings of a modern legal system in 1889 when, under pressure from a popular movement, the Emperor promulgated a constitution which established executive, legislative, and judicial departments. However, each was responsible to him. In particular, 'the judicature shall be exercised by the courts of law according to law, in the name of the Emperor'. The judiciary was subordinated to the executive, with the Ministry of Justice controlling administration of the courts. The 'rights and duties of the subject' were granted only 'within the limits of law'. The constitution itself was to be interpreted by the ordinary courts or the Privy Council, not by the Supreme Court, and to be amended only at the initiative of the Emperor; it was never altered. The courts, however, could not rule on the constitutionality of laws, nor could they pass judgment in disputes between government and citizens.[8]

After defeat in the second world war, Japan was forced to accept an American-designed constitution of quite different character. It placed emphasis on civil liberties, and gave the right to interpret the constitution to the Supreme Court, while amendments were to be initiated by the parliament, or Diet, with an affirmative vote of two thirds of members of both House of Representatives and House of Councillors. The Supreme Court was awarded responsibility for the lower courts, which were made independent of both the executive and the legislature, and given the power to pronounce on the constitutionality of all legislation and administrative action, provided the issue was embodied in law. Judges have tenure, and may not be removed except by impeachment or, in the case of the Supreme Court, through a plebiscite.[9] Rule of law has thus been firmly entrenched; nevertheless, Hiroshi Oda's paper shows that vestiges of arbitrary action by the executive remain as so-called 'administrative guidance'.

Singapore before the second world war was part of the British colony known as Straits Settlements. As was the case throughout the Empire, a firm division was maintained between executive and judiciary. The position of the latter was safeguarded first by the general rule of law that no action could lie against a judge of the Supreme Court for any act done in his judicial capacity. In addition, the Courts Ordinance of 1907 prescribed that no person acting judicially could be sued provided that he at the time believed himself to have jurisdiction to do or order the act of which complaint was made.[10] In brief, in the years before the second world war Singapore was governed under rule of law.

This happy situation was eventually brought to an end by a series of events which was set in train by Japanese occupation, and consequent inflammation of Chinese nationalist feeling. When Britain created the Malayan Union in 1946, it established Singapore as a separate Crown Colony. Emergency Regulations were brought in to contain the Communist uprising then threatening; in 1955 these were replaced by an Internal Security Act (ISA). Singapore obtained self government within the British Commonwealth in 1959, and a year later confirmed the Internal Security Act. In 1963 the city-state became part of Malaysia, but seceded in 1965 and became fully independent. It maintained the ISA, which allows for detention without trial for an indefinitely renewable two-year period. Furthermore, as Andrew Harding's chapter concludes, the courts are subordinate to the executive. One cannot say that Singapore is now under rule of law.[11]

The gradual development of law in Thailand is sketched in some detail by Vitit Muntarbhorn in his contribution to this volume. Suffice it here to emphasize that this is, as elsewhere in Asia, a latter-day phenomenon. In the first half of the 19th century, under King Rama III (1824-1851),

> 'In general, the administration of justice and maintenance of internal security were minimal activities of government ... The government encouraged, directly and indirectly, the settlement of

minor disturbances at the local level. Judicial procedures were time consuming, and the bribing of judges was accepted practice.'[12]

Much the same might be said about indigenous rule in other parts of Asia[13] before the colonial powers imposed a system of courts (Thailand remained independent). To put it briefly, the separation of powers between executive and judiciary, with the latter administering a system of laws which binds all, including the executive, is a Western concept alien to indigenous tradition, where the executive has priority over the judiciary. As Vitit Muntarbhorn shows, in Thailand notions of rule of law were closely tied in with the country's modernization, itself pursued to fend off the colonial powers on Thailand's borders. However, as Asian states in this century have discovered that power and pelf may be achieved without rule of law, so they have felt less induced to follow the Western model of government.

References

1. Jaudel, E. (1990), p. 23.
2. Hinton, H.C. (1963), pp. 19,20,31,33.
3. Furnivall, J.S. (1944), pp. 60,61,67.
4. *Ibid.*, pp. 124,157,159.
5. *Ibid.*, p. 295,296.
6. Kahin, G. M. (1952), p. 53.
7. Furnivall, J.S. (1944), p. 299.
8. Ike, N. (1963), pp. 181,182,198.
9. *Ibid.*, pp. 200.
10. Braddell, R. St John (1982), pp. 122,123.
11. To put matters into perspective, however, it must also be mentioned that the British 'Northern Ireland (Emergency Provisions) Act' in its latest version of 1987 still contains Section 12 which permits 'the security forces in Northern Ireland to detain suspected terrorists indefinitely without charge or trial'. This is 'an executive order which is in all essential respects immune from judicial supervision'. In practice no detention order has been issued since 1975. Finn, J.E. (1991), pp. 92,94. More important, perhaps, is the

fact that apart from this law the judiciary in Britain remain independent of the executive.

12. Vella, W. (1957), p. 17.
13. For an account of the situation before Dutch rule in Aceh (pr. Acheh), at the northwestern tip of the Indonesian island of Sumatra, see Snouck Hurgronje, C. (1906), p. 102.

Party and Law in China

PHILIP BAKER

No one will be surprised to learn that the relationship between the Communist Party and the legal system in China is complex, multi-faceted and remains still largely obscure. I am reminded of a comment made by an ambassador in Peking after the events of June 1989 in and around Tiananmen Square. He said that we know less about the operation of the Chinese Government now than we did in the last years of the reign of the Empress Dowager, Ci Xi, at the turn of the century. In this paper I hope to highlight some of what we know about the relationship between the party and the law, as well as those areas which remain unclear and which would provide fruitful fields for research. (Some of the best research - which provided us with the clearest information about the Communist Party - was the result of interviews with *emigrés* from China in the 1960s. It is surprising that little opportunity is being taken of the recent round of *emigrés* to obtain clear details of how the Chinese state works). In this talk, I shall be focusing on those facets of the relationship relating to legislation and adjudication.

Before I turn to look at China, it may be as well if I set up what I might regard as a paradigm for the relationship between political parties and a legal system. This is based largely upon Western practice, much of which has been inherited by governments of former colonies, who received their constitutions from Western countries. I set up this paradigm in order to throw into sharper contrast where the relationship between party and law in China differs markedly from that which operates in so many other countries.

In this paradigm, the political parties present candidates for election. If elected, a party influences the law primarily via the content of legislation though, in many countries, often after a compromise on the terms of the legislation with other minority parties. Party documents and speeches at party conferences are all aimed towards presenting the policies with a view to gaining election, or with a view to influencing the content of legislation.

The individuals who become judges will have their own personal political views which, together with any association they may have with political parties, may have an influence upon their choice as judges. This may be overt, as in the selection of judicial candidates in the United States, particularly at Supreme Court level, or it may be more discreet, such as the influence in the selection of English judges: Lord Donaldson, for example, was for many years an adviser to the Conservative Party before his appointment to the bench. Once appointed, however, it is assumed that a judge will not act as an appointee of the party with which he was previously associated. This is taken to the point where, for example, English judges sever all links with any political organizations or other representative bodies with which they may have been previously associated.   While the particular political inclinations of an individual judge are likely to influence his decisions, it is assumed and expected that he will show independence. This is ensured by giving him or her security of tenure so that, even if selected because of association with a particular political party, the judge is not in any way subject to coercion by the party.

This paradigm does not necessarily represent the practice in all countries, nor is it necessarily the only possible paradigm. It is, however, an interesting yardstick by which to check the practice in China. No one will be surprised to learn that it departs in several respects from the paradigm; some of the implications of that I leave readers to discern.

History

Before turning to look at the legislative and judicative position in China, it may be helpful to say a brief word about the history of the legal system in modern China.

In spite of the fact that the party has had no trained lawyers amongst its members, I should point out that it had extensive experience of legal administration prior to obtaining control over the entirety of China (minus Taiwan) in 1949. But even prior to that it controlled vast tracts of territory - 'liberated areas', whose earliest legislative texts date from around 1927. In 1931, the party declared the foundation of the Chinese Soviet Republic and began to build up an extensive legal system. It was in the liberated areas that the party first gained experience of drafting legislation and administration of justice. Several practices of Chinese justice originated there; for example, appealing to the 'mass line' in determining cases, the use of people's assessors, and even the systems of administrative detention and of labour camps.

Immediately prior to the foundation of the People's Republic in 1949, the party also did what no other communist party in the world has done (so far as I am aware). It announced the abolition of all pre-existing laws of the Nationalist regime. This was entirely consistent with the Marxist concept of the non-inheritability of law: that law developed under a bourgeois system could not be inherited by a socialist system. Despite that, no other Communist Party appears to have wiped the slate clean in quite the same way.

In February of 1949, in the 'Instructions for Abolishing the KMT's Book of Six Laws and Determining Judicial Principles for Liberated Areas', the party announced that all existing laws were to cease to have effect and that, pending the enactment of new laws, People's Courts should have regard to party policies and other programmes in determining cases.

This was made concrete by Article 17 of the Common Programme, issued on the eve of the declaration of the People's Republic, which provided:

> 'All laws, decrees and judicial systems of the Kuomintang reactionary government that oppress the people shall be abolished. Laws and decrees protecting the people shall be enacted and the people's judicial system shall be established.'

The abolition of all existing laws created a legal vacuum to be filled by laws enacted by the new regime. Pending their enactment, the courts were to have regard to the party's policies in determining cases. In practice, the vacancy that was created has only gradually been filled during the last 45 years; there still remain certain *lacunae* in the legislative system. For example, it was not until 1979 that a criminal code was enacted, and it was only in 1986 that general principles of civil law were enacted. The period of time during which the courts were obliged to have regard to party policies in determining cases was much longer than might originally have been expected. I shall return to the role of the party in determining individual cases later.

Legislation: the party and the legislative system

Turning from this brief history to the legislative system in the People's Republic, I need to say a word first about the existing types and processes of legislation. Under the current Chinese constitution, which dates from 1982, there are three types. Firstly, major laws are enacted by the National People's Congress - China's parliament - either in its annual plenary sessions or at the Standing Committee which meets, on average, about once a month. All major and basic laws are enacted through these bodies.

Secondly, administrative regulations (*xing zheng fa gui*) are enacted by the State Council - the equivalent of a cabinet - and by ministries under the council. To these bodies are sometimes delegated powers to make laws on particular topics (in the 1980s, the NPC Standing Committee delegated powers to enact quasi-legislation on retirement policy, tax reform, economic restructuring and on the open door policy).

Finally, local regulations (*di fang xing fa gui*) are enacted by People's Congresses and People's Governments below national level. There are three levels of local government labelled (for most of the country) provincial, city or county, and township or district levels. These are permitted to adapt national legislation to comply with local circumstances, or adopt other local provisions.

All the major state organs have associate bodies responsible for the drafting of legislation. Thus, for example, the National People's Congress has a Law Committee set up under Article 37 of the Organic Law of the NPC.[1] The Standing Committee of the NPC has a Legislative Affairs Committee.[2] These bodies assist in the drafting and the vetting of national level legislation. The State Council has a Legislative Bureau which was re-established in April of 1986. It fulfils several functions, including the drafting of State Council and ministerial legislation. It has five departments[3] for drafting in particular fields, and a research office.

Turning from state to party organs, the 1982 constitution makes no reference in its body to the Communist Party. However, its Preamble alludes to the 'four cardinal principles' which underpin the entire structure of the PRC, including the party leadership; this is generally regarded as providing the latter with legitimacy.

The party ensures its control over the national and local People's Congresses and over the People's Governments via the nomination and *nomenklatura* systems. Under the first of these, the party nominates candidates for selection to the various People's Congresses. The *nomenklatura* system is based upon that of the former Soviet Union; it ensures that government positions at certain levels are reserved for party members, some by those of specified rank: the party and the state both employ a complex, multi-tier grading for party and state cadres.

Alongside the structure of government - People's Congresses and People's Governments - is a parallel party structure. This is set out in the party constitution (also dating from 1982). At national level, the party is controlled by a Central Committee, which functions through a smaller Politburo; this has a Standing Committee (presently of seven members) which effectively controls the party and governs China. Below the level of the Central Committee, there are party organizations at provincial and county levels and local branches.

The party has legal bodies paralleling the legal committees and legal bureaux of the National People's Congress and the State Council. These are sometimes termed the political and legal departments (*zheng fa bu men*). Details of these party departments are still highly obscure. At Central Committee level, there exists a Politics and Law Leading Group, presided over by a member of the Politburo Standing Committee (until recently, Qiao Shi). At all levels there exist Party Political-Legal Committees (*zheng fa wei yuan hui*) of which more will be said later.

It is far from clear what role these party committees play in the preparation of legislation. Indications are that legislative drafts move backwards and forwards between the various legislative drafting committees of the state organs, and the party political-legal departments and committees. Some drafts may begin with party departments, others with state organs. There are few descriptions of the concrete legislative process[4]; those which exist suggest that the party political-legal departments propose the content of legislation, pass the matter over to the state legislative bodies for drafting, and then review the drafts to ensure conformity with party policy. In many cases, the membership of the state and the party bodies will be overlapping. This is an area upon which we know relatively little and which could very fruitfully be an area for future research.

Aside from the role of state bodies and of party organs in enactment of legislation, there is also a parallel process for production of party documents. These are drafted and redrafted by party bodies at senior levels and are then passed down through party channels. They are studied and acted upon by members at lower levels.

An example can be given from the control of religious activities in China. State legislation requires the registration of all places of religion (State Council Regulations on the Registration of Social Organizations, 13 October, 1989), but this legislation says little or nothing about requirements for registration. Those are, at present, primarily found in several key party documents. A series issued in the late 1980s and 1990s set out the party's policies towards religious activities and bodies.

Apart from exclusive party documents, there are also joint party-state papers. An examination of the 1992 State Council Gazette, for example, reveals the inclusion of a Communist Party Central Committee and State Council joint document on quickening the development of tertiary industry. Similarly, a 1992 Judicial Handbook contains a Central Committee-State Council joint document on Severely Combatting the Theft of Objects from Ancient Graves. There are many similar examples. A volume in my possession of legislation on maintenance of personnel files includes six party documents, three of them joint Central Committee-State Council documents, the rest party-only: they also reveal parallel party and state organizations for maintaining personnel files.

It is by no means clear why a particular normative document is issued with the imprimatur of both the party and state organs. One book on Chinese law[5] suggests that those documents which are of particular relevance to party members are issued jointly. While logical, this does not appear to fit actual practice. The book also suggests that the issue of joint state-party documents is declining;

the examples I have given show that though this may be so, it still continues.

The existence of party and party-state normative documents raises a fundamental question as to the definition of 'legislation' in the People's Republic of China. Are these documents to be regarded as legislation? If so, then we need to have an expansive definition of what constitutes law there. It also challenges us to provide an adequately expansive definition of the concept of law. If we say that law encompasses all normative rules governing the conduct and lives of individuals, it follows that these documents are law. I shall return to this towards the end when I ask the question whether the party is above the law.

Adjudication: the party and the judicial system

Party control over the courts is exercised via the *nomenklatura* system and via the party political-legal committees at all levels parallel with the courts. Under the first system, appointments to certain levels in the courts are reserved for members of the Communist Party. This would include the presiding judge of the courts at each of four levels: the Supreme People's Court at national level, Higher Level People's Courts at provincial level, Intermediate People's Courts at county and city level, and Basic Level People's Courts at the lowest level. In each court there is a presiding judge and several other judges.

At each level of court, there exists a Communist Party political-legal committee or commission. It is understood that this consists of the heads of the equivalent level Public Security Bureau, Procuracy, and People's Court, meeting under the chairmanship of the local party secretary. (The Public Security Bureau represents the ordinary police in China; the Procuracy is responsible, *inter alia*, for prosecuting criminals).

For example, at the party Central Committee level, the political-legal committee (generally called the Political and Legal Commission - PLC) includes the President of the Supreme People's Court, the Minister of Justice and the Minister of Public Security; it is said to provide overall policy guidance on the way law is to be enforced[6]. Its secretary is a key member of the Central Committee Secretariat (formerly Qiao Shi, now Ren Jian-xin).

These political-legal committees first appeared in 1959, in the period following the Anti-Rightist Movement when the legal system was in the descendant and the public security apparatus in the ascendant.[7] So far as is known, the committees do not meet in formal session, nor do they have a specific staff separate from that of the constituent departments. Rather, documents and files of important cases are passed around amongst members of party political-legal committees, who reach agreement on handling of cases. It is widely believed, though far from being proved, that these committees take the decision to prosecute as well as on the outcome of particular cases. Thus these committees will decide whether or not an individual should be arrested, what charge should be brought against him, if and when a trial should be held, whether he is guilty and what should be the ultimate sentence.

These committees have been more or less active at various times in Chinese legal history. After their appearance in 1959 they dominated the legal scene of the early 1960s. With the rebuilding of the legal system after the end of the Cultural Revolution, less was heard about them. It was reported that in September 1979 the party Central Committee issued an instruction abolishing the practice of examination and approval of cases by party committees. This instruction seems never to have been fully followed. In the period of repression since the events of June 1989, these committees have again become prominent. They appear to be the primary mechanism by which the party maintains control over the operation of the entire public security and judicial process.

To highlight one example, on or about 4 July, 1983, the Political-Legal Commission of the party Central Committee held a telephone conference calling upon judicial, procuratorial and public security organs to improve the work of public order. This signalled the commencement of a major law and order campaign, with large numbers of arrests. It is estimated that in the last six months of 1983, 10,000 or more executions took place. We also now have firm evidence that quotas of executions were handed down (through party channels) to each province and then to each individual court. Only on 2 September, 1983, two months after the campaign started, were these steps legitimized through the state apparatus, by the Standing Committee of the NPC when it amended several provisions of the Criminal Code and Criminal Procedure Code.

Two further features of the Chinese courts system also permit greater party control over adjudication. Cases in China are determined not by individual judges but by collegiate decision of the particular court in question. Adjudication committees operate in all courts, and are required to deliberate on and reach a consensual decision on the outcome of cases. In these committees, the dominant role of the presiding judge - generally a party member - will be vital.

Secondly, judges in China enjoy no security of tenure. Under the constitution and under the Organic Laws, judges are appointed and may be removed by the People's Congress or People's Government at the relevant level. It is not unusual for judges to come from other government departments - the army or the procuracy for example, and to be moved on to other posts within the government or the party. A high level example occurred at the party congress last year when Ren Jian-xin, President of the Supreme People's Court since 1988, was appointed Secretary of the Central Committee's Politics and Law Commission (in place of Qiao Shi). Ren came to prominence in the crackdown after Tiananmen; on the afternoon after the massacre he sponsored a Supreme Court telegram to the central government calling the student demonstrations a counter-revolutionary movement; this pre-judged the case of any demonstrator charged with counter-revolutionary crimes. Ren has also expounded the need for legal departments to accept the leadership of the party and has a reputation for ringing up lower court judges and telling them how to decide cases.

The role and functioning of party Political-Legal Committees, the collegiate nature of the Chinese bench, and lack of security of tenure all raise very sharply the issue of independence of the judiciary. The 1982 Constitution of the PRC, in Article 126, states as follows:

> 'The People's Courts exercise judicial power independently, in accordance with the provisions of the law, and are not subject to interference by any administrative organ, public organization or individual.'

A similar provision is found in Article 4 of the Organic Law of the People's Courts.

The inclusion of this guarantee of independence of the judiciary in the 1982 Constitution was by no means uncontroversial.[8] The concept itself came under attack during the Anti-Rightist Movement and the Cultural Revolution as bourgeois; with society subject to the overall leadership of the party, how could there be judicial independence? The inclusion of Article 126 in the 1982 Constitution was therefore an important statement of principle, as was the reference to the courts not being subject to interference by any public organization: it was taken by many in 1982 that this referred specifically to the Communist Party.

It is difficult to reconcile the practice of the party political-legal committees with guarantees of independent exercise of judicial power. An on-going debate in China turns on the difference between involvement of the party in concrete determination of individual cases, and overall guidance by the party in general policy of the courts. Last year, in answer to questions from the British delegation to China led by Lord Howe, Ministry of Public Security officials indicated that party committees on politics and law existed only to give guidance on ideology and structure. It is hard to know whether that distinction is a workable distinction or not. General policy guidance over a body which is required to determine individual cases can easily merge into concrete determination of specific issues.

The question remains whether, given the existence of the party Political-Legal Committees, the *nomenklatura* system, and the role of adjudication committees in People's Courts, there can be such a concept as independence of the judiciary in China.

Is the party above the law?

I turn to a further and final issue, which brings together the role of the party in legislative and judicial matters: whether the party is subject to law or is above it. Article 5 of the 1982 Constitution contained a very pointed statement:

> 'No organization or individual is privileged to be beyond the constitution or the law'.

Again, the inclusion of this provision in 1982 was not uncontroversial, and the reference to 'organization' was again taken by many to refer to the Communist Party. It is open to question whether this principle is observed in practice or not.

One particular, concrete example - trite but perhaps going some way to answering the question - may illustrate. In 1989 an Administrative Litigation Law was enacted which went into force in 1990. This law provides that individuals may challenge before the courts the concrete decisions of administrative organs. The issue has arisen whether a party committee may constitute an administrative organ. A case was brought by Guo Luoji, an academic at Nanjing University, against the university Communist Party Committee. Following the events of 1989, the committee had prevented Guo from publishing or teaching. He sought to challenge their decision before the courts under the Administrative Litigation Law. The court refused to hear the case on the basis that party committees were not administrative organs and were therefore not subject to review.

Given the role that party committees play in the enactment of legislation and in adjudication, it is hard not to reach the conclusion that the organs of the Communist Party are both above law and outside it in every respect. The party is involved in the making of law, not simply by influencing the content of legislation, but also by enacting normative party and joint party-state documents. The party participates (to put it at its lowest) in the concrete determination of individual cases via the appointment and control of judges and the party political-legal committees. The Nanjing Intermediate Court was perhaps right to reject Guo Luo-ji's case, but for the wrong reasons: how can the party judge itself?

References

1. Set up under Article 70 of the constitution, and Article 37 of the Organic Law of the NPC, with one chairman, six vice-chairmen, and eighteen ordinary members.
2. This was originally called the Legislative Committee but was renamed in 1983.
3. Du, X.-C. and Zhang, L.-Y. (1990), p. 59. These are: financial, economic, and foreign trade; agricultural and forestry; industrial and communications; supervisory; political and judicial.
4. One exception concerns the drafting of the Bankruptcy Law.
5. Zheng, H. (1988), p. 10.
6. *Ibid.*
7. One of the best early descriptions of these bodies is Barnett, D. (1967), pp. 194-197.
8. Independence of the judiciary was included in the 1954 constitution, but dropped in 1975 and 1978.

Democracy's Struggle in Indonesia[1]

ADNAN BUYUNG NASUTION

Introduction

A constitutional government is defined by limitation of powers. Therefore, according to Lev,[2] constitutionalism - a somewhat higher abstraction than rule of law or *rechtstaat* - means 'the limited state', where political power is circumscribed by clear laws and where power is transformed into authority limited by law. Constitutionalism implies that 'rule of law' is superior to political power. According to A.A.G. Peters,[3] rule of law functions such that the limitation of power plays a role in ensuring that rational principles guide the making of political decisions. Four norms characterize a constitutional state. These are:

> (1) legality (legal supremacy), as standards to be observed or as affirmative ideals to be pursued;
> (2) the existence of an independent judiciary;
> (3) a guarantee of human rights, including clear procedures for their attainment;
> (4) good governance.

The last two norms serve to guarantee human values in a domestic and external content. The fundamental elements of constitutionalism are the presence of legal limits on power and the responsibility of the government to the governed.[4] In the contemporary world, these two elements are closely related to democracy and human rights. Therefore, sociologically, constitutionalism can be seen as a commitment to limit prevailing political power. And democracy requires a balance between the power of the state and the individual, as well as guarantees on collective rights.[5]

We can use this simple theoretical framework to consider the Indonesian commitment to the idea of constitutional or democratic government. And the historical roots of this commitment can be traced back to and before the proclamation of independence. This was the culmination of the people's movement for liberation from the grip of Dutch colonial government. A spirit of humanism and democracy motivated the proclamation. It loses its significance if interpreted simply in terms of breaking free from foreign domination. This would ignore the fact that underlying the proclamation was a genuine popular urge for liberation from suppression, suffering and all other shackles which cripple humanity. In essence, the real meaning contained in the proclamation of independence touched on the desire for freedom which is felt in the heart of every individual. In other words, the proclamation was about Indonesians as individuals becoming human beings free in soul and mind, independent and in possession of human value and dignity. In my opinion, this essence of the 1945 proclamation of independence should always guide Indonesian national and state life.

In line with the concept of constitutional government, the substantive meaning of the proclamation itself makes the state a tool for liberation of the people. The preamble of the 1945 constitution makes 'promoting the nation's welfare' one aim of the state. This purpose is also clear in the late President Soekarno's address to the Investigating Committee for the Preparation of Indonesian Independence (*BPUPKI* or *Dokuritsu Junbi Coosakai*) (which I shall refer to as the Investigating Committee) on 1 June, 1945, where he argued that national independence was essential if the individual was to be personally freed.

> 'If everyone of the 70 million Indonesian people had to be first free mentally before we could achieve political independence, I repeat, we will not gain an independent Indonesia until

Doomsday! It is within an independent Indonesia that we will liberate our people! It is within an independent Indonesia that we will liberate the hearts of our people.'[6]

The establishment of the Republic of Indonesia on 18 August, 1945 was thus a necessary step towards achieving liberation of the people by making them aware of their sovereignty, rights and obligations. So the upholding of human and citizen rights is very much part of the imperatives implicit in the proclamation of independence. The 1945 constitution - despite its weaknesses (which were recognized by its formulators) - became the basis for regulating the mechanism, tasks, and authority of government administration, as well as for limiting the power of the state so that it did not conflict with popular aspirations. The essential meaning of the proclamation clearly requires the state to create conditions conducive to uplift and to protect the whole nation, meaning that it must uphold the law and respect human rights. In other words, the concept of constitutionalism or democratic government is in line with the spirit and essential meaning of the proclamation of independence.

Interest in the substantive meaning of the proclamation encouraged me to undertake a comprehensive study of the *Konstituante* (Constituent Assembly) which sat from 1956 to 1959, and may be viewed as the culmination of the struggle to establish constitutional government. My study clearly shows that the elected representatives genuinely tried to bring about a constitutional order where the state would be a tool with which the people could achieve their ideals, and where government power would be placed in a constitutional framework which protected human rights. In other words, they attempted to create a constitutional government and very nearly succeeded. The study provides evidence of how widespread, productive and creative was the thinking in favour of constitutional government or, in Herbert Feith's phrase, 'constitutional democracy',[7] among Indonesian political leaders in the 1950s.

However, as the record shows, constitutional government has been far from a reality over the last 30 years. Just as occurred in debates in the Investigating Committee, in the actual practice of government under both 'Old Order' and 'New Order' regimes[8] proposals for constitutional government which protect human rights have been defeated by totalitarian concepts, such as the 'integral state'.[9] However, I am confident that as long as the government neglects aspirations for constitutionalism, the people will continually struggle to achieve them, and in doing so will oppose the ruling regime. The historical facts show that the journey of the Indonesian state, right up to the present, has been characterized by constant 'pushing and pulling' between, on the one hand, the ruling elite who use the theory of the integral state to legitimize themselves and, on the other hand, the aspirations of the general population who want a democratic government.

Roots of the conflict between theories of constitutional government and of the totalitarian state

From the first decade of Indonesia's independence, the struggle for constitutionalism has confronted ideas which can be traced back to the time when the 1945 Constitution was formulated. In sessions of the Investigating Committee, there was a debate on the form to be taken by the independent Indonesian state between those who favoured constitutional government and those who wished to put into practice a totalitarian state philosophy. Soepomo, an expert in customary law, suggested an 'integral state', which was in line with the *gotong royong* (mutual assistance) state proposed by Soekarno, later president. The proposal by Hatta (later vice-president) and Yamin (a prominent nationalist leader), viewed in the light of contemporary constitutional theory, were much closer to the notion of a constitutional government protecting civil and human rights. This initial debate is the historical source for all subsequent discussion and confrontation between proponents of the two ideas, at the level of both discourse and constitutional practice.[10] From the late 1970s, the theory of the integral state has been brought back to prominence by the 'New Order' regime. It may therefore be useful to elaborate it in more detail.

According to Soepomo, there are three theories of the state, namely: 1. individualistic; 2. class based; 3. integral. On this last he argued that:

> 'The integral theory was taught by Spinoza, Adam Mueller, Hegel and others (18th and 19th century). They viewed the function of the state as not being the protection of the interest of an individual or any particular group, but rather as being the safeguarding of the interests of the entire society, as a unity. The state is a structure of an integral society, all groups, all parts and all members are closely related to each other and form an organic social unity. The most important thing for the state based on the integral idea is the life of the nation in its totality. The state does not take sides with the strongest or largest group, does not consider the interests of an individual as its centre. But the state guarantees the security of the life of the nation as an indivisible unity ... The basis of the legal structure in West European countries is individualism and liberalism. This individualist character concerns all fields of life (the systems of laws on economy, art, etc.) separating man from all other associations. All of this always creates imperialism and a system of exploitation, causing chaos and confusion in the physical and spiritual world. Such a character should be kept away from the development of the Indonesian state, even Europe itself is experiencing a tremendous spiritual crisis, because the soul of the European people is tired of the evils which result from such an individualistic spirit ... The basis of the state structure in Soviet Russia at present is the dictatorship of the proletariat. It might be that this basis is in accordance with the specific social conditions in Soviet Russia. But the basic principles underlying this state are in contradiction with the real and original character of Indonesian society.'

To strengthen his proposal, examples were then given of the concepts of the state of Nazi Germany and of *Dai Nippon* (Japan), of which Soepomo approved. He argued that these were based on the totalitarian school of thought, '*das Ganze der politischen Einheit des Volkes*' [the complete unity of the people]. In both Nazi Germany and Japan, there were characteristics which Soepomo, as an expert in customary law, very much admired and wished to see in the new state. These were the unity between leader, state, and people; the spirit of unity;   and the family principle. Soepomo further argued:

> 'The *Fuhrung* [leadership] principle as *Kernbegriff* [basic idea] of *ein totaler Fuhrerstaat* [a state under absolute leadership] ... was the principle of the similarity, and the shared territory, between the leadership and the people. From the national socialist stream of thought (Germany), the principle of unity between the leadership and the people, and the principle of the unity within the whole nation are in accordance with the Eastern way of thinking ...
>
> *Dai Nippon* is based on the eternal, physical and spiritual unity between the Supreme Highness *Tenno Heika*, the state and the Japanese people as a whole. The *Tenno* is the spiritual centre of the whole people. The state rests upon the family principle. The Tenno family is called *Koshitsu*, the paramount family. This unity and family principle is also very much in accordance with the character of the society.'

The unity of leader and people on the Nazi model and the *Dai Nippon* family principle were considered appropriate for Indonesian society. Soepomo further explained:

> 'The inner spirit, the spiritual structure of the Indonesian people aspires to the unity of life, the unity of *kawulo* and *gusti* (servant and master), that is, the unity between the external and spiritual world, between microcosm and macrocosm, between the people and their leaders. Every individual, every group of human beings in a society and all communities in social intercourse throughout the entire world, all have their respective place and duty in life *(dharma)*, according to their natural fate, and everything is directed to an external and spiritual balance. Every human being

as an individual cannot be separated from other individuals or from the external world, from groups of humanity, even from all classes of creatures, everything is all mixed up, connected, all mutually influencing each other, with lives interconnected. This is the totalitarian idea, the idea of the integral Indonesian nation ...'

The key word in Soepomo's concept of the state is 'totalitarian', as practised in Nazi Germany. This was then combined with his obsession for unity and the family principle as in *Dai Nippon* under *Tenno Heika*. However, Soepomo provided a justification for his theories by referring to what he called 'the original, indigenous Indonesian form of government':

'According to the nature of the indigenous Indonesian form of government, which can still be observed in villages in Java, Sumatra and other Indonesian islands, state officials are leaders who are spiritually united with the people, state officials are always obliged to hold firmly to unity and balance in their society. The village head or leader of the people is obliged to act upon an awareness of justice for the people, must always give form *(Gestaltung)* to the feeling of justice and to the aspirations of the people. Therefore, the leader of the people is "loyal to *adat* [custom]" (in the words of a saying of the Minangkabau,[11] always pays attention to developments in society, and for that purpose, always consults *(bermusyawarah)* with the people or with the head of families in his village. This is in order that the spiritual ties between the leader and the people may always be maintained. In an atmosphere of unity both between the people and their leader, and between the various groups in the community, all groups are united by the spirit of *gotong-royong* and *kekeluargaan* (family spirit).
    It is thus clear ... that if we want to establish the Indonesian state in accordance with the unique character and form of Indonesian society, the state should be based on the idea of the integral state, the state which is united with the whole people, which is above all groups in whatever field.'

With such a philosophy, Soepomo thought it did not matter what form of state - monarchy or republic - was chosen. He did not consider this a basic principle of government structure. The important thing was that the head of state, and indeed all government agencies, were characterized by their leadership of the state and the whole people. The title of the head of state did not matter; he could be even 'His Excellency the Ruler' - the important thing was that he should be a true leader. 'He should be united in soul with the whole people. This is regardless of whether we will appoint a head of state with hereditary rights, or only for a limited period'. It would be preferable not to elect a leader or head of state as do Western democracies, because that method is based on individualism.

Soepomo's theory greatly emphasizes the government's role, and especially that of the head of state. In terms of modern government theory, it implies 'a concentration of responsibility and power in government'. However, it was in line with Soekarno's concepts of state and government. Although Soekarno never used the term 'integral state', he used terms such as 'state based on *gotong royong*', and *Nasakom* (an acronym from the Indonesian for nationalism, religion and communism), an amalgamation of all revolutionary forces.[12] All of these reflected Soekarno's obsession concerning the unity and integrity of society under the protection of an Indonesian state. Rhetorically, Soekarno described 'a mutual cooperation state' as a dynamic concept, more dynamic than the 'family concept'. 'The family concept', he said, 'is a static concept.'[13] But, although he did not favour the term, his actions were as totalitarian as Soepomo's. This became particularly obvious when he put into force his concept of 'Guided Democracy' between 1959 and 1965. These two prominent figures both tended to argue from the stand-point of an 'original Indonesian society'. So when formulating the 1945 constitution, their thinking supported one another. Matters were different with Hatta and Yamin. These two prominent figures did not reject collectivism, but they could not accept Soepomo's theory of the totalitarian state. Indeed, Hatta later revised the concept of collectivism, of which he approved, by inserting into it the principle that political decisions, following a process of *musyawarah* [consultation], should be made by majority vote.[14] Hatta also could not approve Soepomo's proposal to give the state and its head a dominant position, which would automatically result in neglect of the rights of citizens, including human rights.[15] He emphasized:

> 'We should pay attention to the necessary conditions to ensure that the state we will establish does not become a state based on power ... Let us not give unlimited power to the state. Therefore it would be best that, in one of the articles such as that on citizenship, in addition to rights already granted, it should be stated also that no citizens should be afraid to express themselves. The rights to associate and assemble or to correspond and so on also need to be stated here. ... This guarantee is necessary to ensure that our state there is not become one based on power, because we are basing our state on the sovereignty of the people. But the people's sovereignty can be used by the state, moreover according to the present draft constitution, the people's sovereignty is vested in the *MPR* [People's Consultative Assembly] and power delegated to the president. The president should not be able to create a state based on power. Thus although we greatly value our great conviction and desire to design a new state, it would be advantageous to provide guarantees to the people, namely the right to freedom of thought. This may appear to have a scent of individualism, but as I said earlier, it is not individualism. Also, in collectivism, there are a few rights to family members to express their feelings, to make the collective body as good as possible. My proposal is only to see that the state we are establishing is not a state of officials, so that afterwards such a state should not become a state based on power, an oppressor state. The basis we suggested is of mutual cooperation and common effort.'

Soepomo objected to this proposal on the grounds that it would introduce double standards into the constitution. He emphasized that he did not accept individualism; the question of possible violations by the government of the rights of the individual to associate or assemble only showed suspicion towards the state. Such a question was individualist in character. If the proposal was included, even though it incorporated only the rights to associate and to assemble, the constitution would embrace two conflicting systems. Such a provision would reflect individualist ideas, and so contradict the basic concept of the constitution. This he considered impermissible.

Furthermore, according to Soepomo, an integral state is like a human body. Different parts of the body cannot hurt one another but must cooperate; so also with the state. Therefore such a state would not require a guarantee of human rights, which are liberal in nature and of Western origin. A guarantee would reflect distrust, lack of confidence and suspicion of the state. Nevertheless, despite Soepomo's obstinacy in opposing Hatta's arguments, they were accepted by the plenary session of the Investigating Committee, as can be seen in the 1945 Constitution itself. Indeed, as well as the right of citizens (Articles 27, 30 and 31), the rights of all residents (including non citizens) are also covered, as set down in Articles 28, 29 and 34.[16]

During voting in the Committee on 10 July, 1945, majority votes were obtained for a republican constitution and for popular sovereignty. This latter principle is clearly quite different from that of the integral state. As such, it is not correct to argue that Soepomo's conceptions fully inspired the 1945 Constitution, its main body as well as its elucidations. This is especially the case with regard to the preamble, in the formulation of which Soepomo was not involved at all. The final draft of the 1945 Constitution owes nothing to his ideas. For reasons unclear, Soepomo himself never again proposed the 'integral state'. When involved, in 1949, in drafting the Constitution of the Federated Republic of Indonesia (RIS) and the (Provisional) Constitution of 1950, Soepomo was a very strong supporter of human rights. These two constitutions were very democratic and contained articles safeguarding human rights. The 1950 Constitution even specified the rights to strike and to demonstrate.

Constitutional government during Indonesia's first decade

The Republic of Indonesia was established on 18 August, 1945 on the basis of popular sovereignty, meaning that it embraced democracy; recognized the principles of rule of law; and aimed at achieving social justice. These three aspirations are very strongly expressed in the 1945 Constitution, although they are formulated in a very brief and simple form. For a new state it was difficult to realize the aspiration for a constitutional government. However, if we carefully study the history of the state from 1945 to 1949, the early phase of the first decade of Indonesia's independence, we can see that starting slowly but surely, the leaders of the community at that time became for the greater part committed to these three aspirations, and genuinely strove for the realization of a truly democratic state.

The principle of constitutional government was clearly put into effect by the Sjahrir cabinet, which replaced the Soekarno-Hatta presidential cabinet, the first formed after the independence proclamation and based on Soekarno's ideas, and which proved ineffective. This was because, firstly, the cabinet consisted mainly of bureaucrats known to have collaborated with the Japanese. Secondly, government authority was clearly concentrated in the hands of the president. Thirdly, Soekarno himself still obeyed the Japanese military government, so that the cabinet was cynically called the *Bucho* Cabinet. Younger nationalists, especially those around Sjahrir, wanted a government embodying the principle of popular sovereignty, and believed that from the outset government should be accountable to the people's representatives in the *KNIP* (Central Indonesian National Committee), the temporary house of representatives. Soekarno, on the contrary, concentrated authority in his own hands. In an attempt to unite the people, he established a state party which involved prominent figures from all political streams. Discontent among youth mounted when the nationalist leader Kasman Singodimedjo, in an address at the inauguration of the *KNIP* on 29 August, 1945, said that the *KNIP* 'was willing to accept all orders from the government'.[17] The *KNIP* was formed to assist the president in running the government prior to the formation of a house of representatives. However it should not have been so subservient because as a provisional parliament it also possessed and should have used a control function *vis-à-vis* the government.

Sjahrir, supported by the youth and Hatta, who was vice president, then succeeded in limiting Soekarno's authority. This success was achieved through several tactical moves inspired by the youth. Their first step was successfully to persuade Sjahrir to become a *KNIP* member. Later he became chairman replacing Kasman Singodimejo. This was Sjahrir's first governmental function in independent Indonesia. His disappointment in Soekarno and Hatta, because they had not proclaimed independence in a way which was totally free from Japanese influence, disappeared when he saw how the proclamation had stimulated the people's spirit and created national unity, as he recorded in his booklet *Out of Exile*.[18] But of course, his actions were based principally on his commitment to uphold democratic principles in the state, in the struggle for which he had participated.

In a political phamplet, *Perjoeangan kita* [Our struggle], Sjahrir sketched the national and international situation, discussing fascism and imperialism, and what should be democratization of the government, making the state a tool to liberate the people, improvement of social and economic conditions and cleansing the Indonesian people from the influence of feudalism, fascism and imperialism. For Sjahrir, a democratic system - as formulated by Soedjatmoko[19] - would enhance Indonesia's long-term ability to fight the enemy, namely all forms of feudalism and the fascism inherited from the Japanese military. And for him, a state, including the Indonesian, could not be an aim in itself, but was rather an expression and tool of popular sovereignty. Indeed it was the most important means for achieving the principal aims, namely freedom, social justice and basic rights. The clear vision in Sjahrir's brochure raised the spirits of the young generation and intellectuals and encouraged them to change the situation. Sjahrir's vision became a clear guide for altering the way in which government was run through the *KNIP*. With the support of Hatta in the government[20] and the youth, in less than two months Sjahrir through the *KNIP* succeeded in effecting a change in the form of government. On 16 October, 1945 Government Decree No. X was issued. This granted legislative power to the *Badan Pekerja* [Working Group] of the *KNIP* (*BP-KNIP*). It was meant to reduce the authority accumulated in presidential hands.

Also, on the proposal of the *BP-KNIP*, on 3 November the government issued a statement permitting and encouraging the formation of political parties.[21] This abolished the state party which had been formed on 23 September and the political system shifted from monoparty to multiparty. The strategic value of this change, as noted by Soedjatmoko, was that it increased the possibility of obtaining support from, and active participation by, the diverse ideological groupings in the community. It was far better suited to this than the one party system.[22] In a democracy, parties are a concrete expression of political currents in the community.[23] By 1951 27 parties were registered, grouped into four streams on the basis of their principles: religious, nationalist, Marxist and ethnic.[24]

The proposal to change the presidential cabinet into a parliamentary one, as pointed out by Pringgodigdo,[25] was also approved by President Soekarno, then holding the highest power in the state before the formation of the *MPR* [*Majelis Permusyawaratan Rakyat* or People's Consultative Assembly). On 15 November, Sjahrir was asked to form a cabinet accountable to the provisional parliament.[26] These changes implied that the constitution had to be formally altered to provide for parliamentary government.[27] The agenda of constitutional change became a constant government concern right up to 1955, when a parliament and a constituent assembly were elected.

The change from presidential to parliamentary cabinet should be noted as a rapid development in the Indonesian constitution, which had crucial strategic meaning. Firstly, it showed that a democratic state could take root on Indonesian soil, when the state was very young, when many obstacles were being faced, and when there was a foreign threat, with the colonial power attempting to return. This should be a continuing example for this country's democratic development, including methods for democratic change. Secondly, this change laid the framework for applying the concept of constitutional government. Its principles, namely the limitation of power and government accountability, were put into effect by the first Sjahrir cabinet and applied by all succeeding governments until the demise of parliamentary democracy in 1957.

In this period, the *KNIP* as a legislative body was relevant and functional. It not only made laws but also controlled the government and had the authority to question all instructions to the people. Governmental power was limited because it was controlled by a popular representative body. This constitutes a very important principle of constitutional government. If a government fails to perform its duty and carry out its programme, according to provisions provided by laws and prevailing political conventions and standards, it should be accountable for such failings, and be replaced.

From that time, the principle of popular sovereignty; of accountability of government to the people; of parties as political organizations and channels for popular aspiration; and of human rights have all constituted real experiences in Indonesia's political history. Sjahrir's cabinet recognized rights of ownership in the territory of the republic and declared that all foreign property would be returned, except when confiscated by the state with compensation. All this was an example not only of respect for fundamental rights but also of applying the principles of good government. And so a democratic government came into operation.

Although in the period 1945-1949 cabinets kept changing, the system was able to survive. After the first Sjahrir cabinet fell, it was successively replaced by his second and third, to be followed in 1947 with one led by Amir Sjarifudin. This did not last long as its Renville Agreement with the Dutch met with widespread rejection. The next cabinet was headed by Hatta, and survived until 1949, when Indonesia obtained full sovereignty and recognition by the international community, including the Netherlands. The constitution then changed from unitary to federal, embodied in the *Republik Indonesia Serikat* [Federated Republic of Indonesia], or *RIS*.

There were several crises at this time. These included the kidnapping of Sjahrir on 3 July, 1946 by supporters of the largest opposition group of the time, led by Tan Malaka,[28] the armed struggle against the Allies, who sought to restore Dutch colonial authority, and the *PKI* (*Partai Komunis Indonesia* or Indonesian Communist Party) revolt in Madiun in 1948, aimed at seizing government. Behind Tan Malaka's opposition movement, from his thinking and teaching I discern a totalitarianism opposed to constitutional government. However, his ideas differed from Soepomo's integral state theory. The latter's argument was more of a cultural character and viewed the state and the people as a single whole, while the people were united with the head of state. Tan Malaka's totalitarianism reflected the Marxist concept of putting all popular forces under one command, not shunning the toppling of government by force. Nevertheless, democratic government survived during the armed revolutions from 1945 until the end of 1949 and thereafter.

The federal constitution of 1949 lasted only eight months before being changed back to a unitary (provisional) constitution in 1950. However, the parliamentary system of government continued until 1956; it therefore lasted more than a decade. The duration of a cabinet in this period depended on its support by the *DPR* (*Dewan Perwakilan Rakyat*, people's representative council, or parliament).[29] Feith considered that the eight governments beginning with the Hatta Cabinet (1949-1950) up to the second Ali Sastroamidjojo cabinet (1957) might be characterized as democratic. He used the phrase 'constitutional democracy'. Among characteristics of the system in this period were the dominant role played by civilians, the very great importance of parties, respect by contenders for power for the 'rules of the game' which were closely related to the prevailing constitution, the fact that the most members of political elite had some sort of commitment to constitutional democracy, civil liberties were rarely infringed, and finally, coercion was avoided.[30]

There were of course a number of failures to maintain the standards of democracy. Governments at this time were never stable. Nevertheless, despite the frequent changes of cabinet, political leaders consistently maintained constitutional government, although they faced regional unrest and revolt, such as the *Darul Islam* [Abode of Islam] rebellion in West Java and Aceh, a revolt in South Sulawesi, and others which emerged in 1953. These were not minor crises because their material and psychological impacts on society were considerable. However, the attempt was made to have a parliament which truly gave effect to the principle of popular sovereignty by organizing general elections in 1955. It is indisputable that these first general elections for the House of Representatives and for the Constituent Assembly were fair, free and secret. To the surprise of many, they produced only four major parties. These were the *PNI* (*Partai Nasional Indonesia*, or Indonesian Nationalist Party), the *Masjumi* (*Majelis Syuro Muslimin Indonesia* or Modernist Muslim Party), the *NU* (*Nahdlatul Ulama*, or Islamic Scholars Party) and the *PKI* (*Indonesian Communist Party*).[31] These elections were historical milestones in the history of the republic. They greatly strengthened the recently built democratic base, as noted by Compton. The multiparty political system with free general elections was in accordance with the demands of a diverse society.[32]

However, after 10 years of this system problems had become very serious. In 1956 and 1957 Indonesia faced a national crisis as a consequence of regional discontent which reached its peak with the *PRRI/Permesta* rebellion (*PRRI* stood for *Pemerintahan Revolusioner Republik Indonesia* or Revolutionary Government of the Republic of Indonesia, while *Permesta* was an acronym for *Perjuangan Semesta* or Overall Struggle). This resulted from economic imbalances between centre and regions and the ensuing dissatisfaction,[33] as well as from discontent within the army. The emergence of the PKI as a significant force was also quite disturbing to the Moslem Group (*Masjumi* and *NU*). All these factors affected political stability. The economy declined sharply. Those who were dissatisfied with the system of parliamentary government, including the army and President Soekarno, blamed the troubles on the party-based governments which they considered incapable. Soekarno, who for the last 10 years had not had real power, from 1956 began to criticize the parliamentary democratic system more intensely. He used a cultural argument: 'Democracy for the last 10 years has been borrowed from other countries and clearly is not satisfying Indonesian society, because it is not in line with the soul of the Indonesian people.' In 1957, he put forward what is known as the 'presidential concept', namely 'guided democracy'. He proposed that government be in the hands of a mutual-cooperation cabinet which would contain representatives of all parties, and that a national council be formed in which all existing groups and streams in the community, including the armed forces, would be represented. The council's task was to advise the cabinet, whether requested or not.

Soekarno's concept was used by the army as an argument to become further involved in politics. Political and economic developments greatly impeded the Constituent Assembly (*Majelis Konstituante*) from doing its work.[34] Since 1952 the army had been demanding dissolution of parliament, so the demise of constitutional government after the second Ali Sastroamidjojo cabinet resigned in March 1957 may be described as a political victory for the armed forces. This was even more clearly the case when Soekarno thereafter declared a state of war and emergency, placed power throughout the country in military hands,[35] and appointed 'Soekarno as citizen' to form a cabinet. Djuanda, a non-party technocrat, was instructed to form a 'working cabinet'.[36]

Deliar Noer[37] gives a comprehensive description of political dynamics and processes of forming of governments, and the concepts, visions and conflicts of political parties, especially the Muslim parties, in the course of Indonesia's political history from 1945 to 1965. This book is an important source, supplementing Feith's classic work[38] for the period 1949 to 1957.

The constitutional governments of this period have been much criticized by their successors, under Soekarno as well as Soeharto, for being based on a political system not in accordance with the nation's identity. However, if this were true, then constitutional government would certainly have been abandoned during the revolution against the Dutch. This is especially so given that at that time the centre of government was in Jogyakarta, the prime centre of feudal Javanese culture. Our leaders were nevertheless able to maintain a democratic system of government. Differences of opinion, even conflicts, existed between government and opposition regarding policies, but this is normal in democratic governments throughout the world, which recognize pluralism in the community. The important thing is that conflicts are resolved by constitutional means through democratic procedures.

More important than cultural factors which of course have some influence, socio-economic conditions were less than supportive for the development of constitutional democracy. At the time, Indonesians hoped that given five to seven years of freedom and independence, prosperity would be achieved. This was of course unduly optimistic. The 'Old Order' regime - and the military right down to the present day - put the blame on parliamentary democracy for the failure of development and the economic decline of the 1950s. This is quite dubious, for as shown in my study[39] the economic deterioration of the 1950s, especially in the period leading up to the Decree of 5 July, 1959 cannot be isolated from preceding conditions. The global crisis of the 1930s struck the Netherlands East Indies heavily, while its entire economic infrastructure was gravely damaged by the fighting during World War II. The subsequent revolt against the Dutch, which lasted about five years, made matters worse. Railways, plantations and other facilities were ruined. All this of course reduced national resources. Therefore, when sovereignty was obtained in 1950, the government inherited a very dire situation, and a period of five to seven years was far too short for any kind of government to achieve substantial improvement. The expectation that prosperity would be attained in so short a time was unduly optimistic. In brief, the socio-economic conditions of the 1950s were not propitious for an experiment in parliamentary democracy.

The Constituent Assembly as the summit of aspirations for constitutional government and the tragic setback

Despite the gravity of the national crisis in the years 1956 to 1959, a democratic debate took place in the Constituent Assembly, in which almost all socio-political groups of the time consistently demanded the continued existence of a democratic parliamentary system. I have three main reasons for regarding the assembly as the summit of aspirations for constitutional government. Firstly, it was a forum for deliberation by representatives from all political streams, religions and faith, with or without party affiliation, throughout Indonesia. These representatives were elected democratically. Secondly, the methods used to elect officials of the assembly to positions in its various subordinate bodies, such as the committees for formulating the constitution, were democratic, as were the actual running of the sessions and the making of decisions. Thirdly, the representatives spoke frankly and without any fear argued in democratic fashion their political interests and options according to their ideological or religious convictions, while in principle being willing to compromise. It became very clear that the majority desired democracy as framework for political life, and constitutional government which could protect the human rights of all citizens.

Surprisingly, very few students of Indonesian political and legal affairs, including Indonesianists, have intensively observed or deeply studied the assembly. This is understandable because both succeeding governments have since viewed it as unproductive and ending in ideological deadlock. Viewed in terms of the democratic aspirations expressed by the proclamation of independence, and the struggle to bring about constitutional government, as provided for by the provisional constitution, the Constituent Assembly had been fulfilling its mandate to formulate a constitution which truly reflected popular aspirations. However, the assembly cannot be viewed in isolation from the political dynamics of the time, from the formulation of the 1945 Constitution right through the period of constitutional government during the first decade of the Republic. This mandate was reflected in Soekarno's message when assembly members were installed on 19 November, 1956, 'Compose a constitution which will make the whole people happy!'; in other words one which would guarantee the safety and prosperity of the people, freedom of religion and human rights.[40]

The assembly lasted from 19 November, 1956 until it was dissolved on 5 July, 1959. Its 474 members represented about 30 political parties and independent groups, so by and large it reflected all groupings active in the community; it included representatives even from Irian Barat (now Irian Jaya), which did not yet form part of the country. In line with the constitution, its members worked hard to deliberate and formulate, in accordance with popular demands, the form, organization and structure of the state as well as human rights of citizens. Through their representatives, the Indonesian people made clear their desire to maintain and further improve a political system based on democracy and constitutionalism, by drafting a better constitution which would be more democratic and provide more guarantees for human rights. At the same time, there was also a desire to correct shortcomings in the political system. For example, in debates concerning the model of democratic government to be chosen, while the concept of constitutional government was broadly accepted, there was a search for a new model where the position of government would be stronger, to avoid the frequent changes of cabinet which had occurred. In other words, the assembly was seeking a better system of government.

A constitutional government need not necessarily take the form of one which can be toppled at any time by parliament. There is a choice between models of accountable government as well as of presidential systems. Between the two poles of a parliamentary government which can be dismissed at any time if the majority withdraws its support, and the presidential system of the United States in which government is guaranteed a specified tenure, there are many possibilities which accord with popular aspirations without losing democratic substance. Experience elsewhere shows that the model of government chosen by a particular country always results from a struggle between contending opinions. The Indonesian people certainly needed a stronger model of government, but one still within a framework of constitutional democracy. This was what was actually being sought and formulated in the assembly.

Unfortunately the debates, especially on ideological options, were considered too long-winded by president and army so that the assembly was not allowed to finish its task. In 1959 the president (backed by the army) proposed a return to the 1945 Constitution. This must be seen against the background of increased tension in government and country, confronted by regional turbulence and, last but not least, the development of Soekarno's ideas, outside the assembly, of 'Guided Democracy'. Nevertheless, the assembly did succeed in completing 90 per cent of its assigned tasks. A number of final agreements were reached on the flag, form of state, and national anthem, as well as on provisions based on popular sovereignty, including restrictions on the executive based on a formulation of human rights. Agreement was reached on 32 items on basic rights and 13 items on civil rights.[41] Of the rights on which final agreement was not reached, categorized differences and similarities in representatives' views had already been placed within a framework of searching for agreement.[42] One matter for pride is that the human rights discussed - including political, economic, social and cultural rights - were more comprehensive than, for example, those set down in the Universal Declaration of Human Rights of 1948.

The assembly had great concern for human rights; for a constitutional government they are a standard which limits its authority. Such government presupposes the existence of specific legal provisions to make it accountable to the institutions of popular sovereignty (in Indonesia, the Parliament, or *DPR*, and the People's Consultative Assembly, or *MPR*). Without such accountability, both popular sovereignty itself, and any restrictions on authority, are meaningless and easily manipulated, as was stipulated by the assembly in the debate on Soekarno's proposal to return to the 1945 Constitution.[43] The crucial matter which it had not decided during its previous meetings was that of state philosophy; this proved to be a major obstacle to achieving majority decision. Yet the question was not insoluble. After three separate votes, neither the supporters of *Pancasila* (the Indonesian official ideology), nor those of Islam could obtain the 316 votes (two thirds of the 474 members) necessary to either reject or approve either as the state philosophy.[44] Wilopo was making efforts to persuade the Muslim group to change their attitude and a compromise seemed not impossible, but General Nasution, the army chief of staff, and supporters of Soekarno, such as Roeslan Abdulgani (Deputy Chairman of the National Council) prevailed on the Muslims to accept an unconditional return to the 1945 Constitution. This was then decreed on 5 July, 1959.

It is nevertheless quite wrong to say that the assembly had failed. Its demise was due to intervention by the army which, as admitted by Nasution[45], had wanted to impose the 1945 Constitution to ensure a strong executive and weaken the influence of political parties. My study mentioned above argues that external factors, especially President Soekarno and the army, sealed the fate of the Assembly and its attempts to draft a new constitution.

The structure and justification of authoritarian government

Feith's term 'decline' is an apt description of political life outside the Constituent Assembly in the 1950s, resulting in its dissolution in 1959. Both Soekarno's 'Old Order' as well as Soeharto's 'New Order' became even more removed from constitutional government. There are several similarities between these two regimes in their methods of legitimating their totalitarian authority. Basing themselves on the 1945 Constitution, they argued that liberal democracy meant Western democracy and that this was not fitted to the conditions and character of Indonesian society. The appropriate democracy would be rather one drawn from Indonesian culture. Soekarno imposed 'Guided Democracy', and Soeharto has based his regime on '*Pancasila* Democracy'. Soekarno's regime was formed in consequence of the 'Return to the 1945 Constitution' decree. Soeharto's regime was originally meant to be a total correction of the previous regime's deviation from that constitution. The slogans formulated were that the ideological base of the 'New Order' is *Pancasila*, the 1945 Constitution is the basis of the system of government, and standards of genuine dedication to the public interest would be upheld.[46] Yet, if both regimes are studied carefully it becomes clear that the 1945 Constitution was interpreted by both regimes mainly to serve their own interests.

In his speech of 17 August, 1959, Soekarno described that year as the 'rediscovery of the revolution'. This idea served as the basis for all political action and policies under 'Guided Democracy', which formally lasted about six years, from the end of the 1959 to 1965. His government still used a cabinet system led by a prime minister, but Soekarno was deeply involved in daily governmental affairs. His government combined three main supporting forces: nationalists (*PNI*), religion (*NU*) and communism (*PKI*). Yet, due to the skill and intelligence of its leader, Aidit, the *PKI* became more and more influential, having a symbiotic relationship with Soekarno. He needed the revolutionary spirit of the communist party, especially towards the end of his rule when he used it to counterbalance the army. At the same time, the *PKI* used Soekarno as an umbrella to strengthen its base and influence, starting within the bureaucracy, including the army, right down to worker and peasant organizations. With its obsession of uniting the people with the state, this regime emerged as repressive and totalitarian.

'Guided Democracy' was first proposed when the 'President's Concept' was announced in February 1957. At that time Soekarno expressed his hope that there could be created a democracy with an Indonesian character, based more on consensus than on the divisive western model with competition between government and opposition in parliament.[47] Then, in front of the Constituent Assembly on 22 April, 1959, he reiterated his idea that liberal democracy should not be imported and adopted because it was not in accordance with the nation's soul, spirit and identity:

> 'Indonesian democracy should be guided or guided democracy, so it will not rest upon the concepts of liberalism ... the democracy we have been using so far is Western democracy, call it parliamentary democracy.'

In his speech of 17 August, 1961, he repeated the same theme: 'Our democracy is not one of free-fight-liberalism. Our democracy is guided democracy ... not a numbers contest in voting'.[48] The key word in Soekarno's concept was 'leadership'.[49] The stress on 'true indonesian identity', consultation, consensus and unity, the rejection of western democracy, liberalism and individualism all appear also under the 'New Order' regime with its use of the term *'Pancasila* Democracy', described as being like that found in traditional villages of Java, West Sumatra, etc. State authority encompasses government, legislature, judiciary, and reform, the maintenance of security and prosperity and so on, and also is free to intervene in community and individual affairs, without discrimination between public and private spheres. The aim is to preserve the unity of society, and to favour life in peace and harmony, in contrast with a system based on competing parties.[50] (A similar view has been presented on various occasions by Koentjaraningrat, a leading anthropologist.) This assumes that ('Western') democracy is suitable only for Western society, and is in basic conflict with Indonesia political ideas. It could bring only disorder, individualism, egoism and materialism. Although Soekarno never referred to the 'integral state', the Soeharto regime to legitimate its authority has since the early 1970s explicitly applied Soepomo's theory. Moreover, the substance and implication of its policies are clear: totalitarianism, neglect of human rights and the concentration of power in the hands of one man, the president. The consequence is the rejection of universal human rights, while 'community interest' - as defined by the regime - is given absolute priority. Open conflict is considered improper; policy very much depends on 'the wisdom of the leader'.

During the period of 'Guided Democracy', Soekarno assumed leadership of all the highest state institutions: the *DPA* (*Dewan Pertimbangan Agung* or Supreme Advisory Council), the *MA* (*Mahkamah Agung*, or Supreme Court), the *DPR*, and *ABRI* (*Angkatan Bersenjata Republik Indonesia* or Armed Forces).

Toward the end of his rule, he made all the leading executives of these institutions into his assistants (in a 'Cabinet of 100 ministers'). As president he appointed and dismissed the appointive members of the *MPR* and the *DPR*. They therefore did not have the courage to use their prescribed right to make the president answerable. With such *MPR* members it is no surprise they appointed Soekarno president for life. Before the people, Soekarno acted as the protecting 'father'. He used the metaphor of the family and the 'spirit of *gotong royong*' to mobilize the people for what he called 'completing the revolution'. He also declared himself protector and spokesman of the people.

Soekarno declared a revolutionary situation and those who were not in line with his wishes were accused of being counter-revolutionary. In this situation law became merely a cover for arbitrary administration and misrule. For example, Soekarno issued Presidential Decree No. 11 of 1953 which was aimed at 'crushing' subversion in order to safeguard the revolution; this constituted a clear violation of rule of law. The revolution became the supreme measuring rod. Everything was said to be done for the revolution. Law No. 19 of 1964 gave authority to the president to intervene in the judiciary if necessary to defend the interests of the revolution. Many political prisoners, including a number of opposition leaders, were imprisoned without trial. Parties were suppressed, and the *Masjumi* and Socialist Parties were dissolved and several of their leaders imprisoned.

Both regimes adopted policies designed to direct and control public opinion. Soekarno's regime stimulated mass enthusiasm to liberate West Irian, to complete the revolution, and to build a spirit of cooperation against the *Nekolims* (neocolonialists). The 'New Order', on the other hand, began by crushing communism, proclaiming economic development, indoctrinating its ideology of *Pancasila*, promoting the 'family spirit' (*semangat kekeluargaan*), and revitalizing Soepomo's integral state theory. The technique used by the 'Old Order' was the mobilization for revolutionary purposes of the people's spirit and enthusiasm. The 'New Order' has made economic development its goal, tranquillized the people with spurious democratic institutions and 'democratic fiestas'. Soeharto has used *Pancasila* and the 1945 Constitution in very obvious fashion as a tool for removing those he dislikes.

The 'New Order' regime has been built on a coalition between bureaucrats, technocrats and the military, all of whose positions have been made stable and permanent. Politics has been managed by intelligence and security agencies such as *Bakin* (*Badan Koordinasi Intelejen Negara* or State Intelligence Co-ordination Board), *Kopkamtib* (*Komando Pemulihan Keamanan dan Ketertiban* or Command for the Restoration of Security and Order), etc. Popular participation in politics is limited. The law has been treated as a tool to legitimize the political and economic policy of the regime.[51] Originally, the 'New Order' was to be established in a spirit of modernization, with the object of total reform in the social, political and economic fields. The positive political developments which took place between 1966 and 1968 did not last long. Under the banner of political reform and economic development, Soeharto carried out a policy of simplifying the political parties. Factions which genuinely desired pro-democracy political reform, such as sections of *KAMI* (*Kesatuan Aksi Mahasiswa Indonesia* or Student Action Front) and *KASI* (*Kesatuan Aksi Sarjana Indonesia* or Indonesian Scholars Action Front) were, within a few weeks of Suharto's assumption of formal power in 1967, pushed aside by factions which had from the outset been in pursuit of power for its own sake and were inspired by men surrounding Soeharto, like his personal assistant Lieutenant General Ali Murtopo.

The military were used to guard against possible disturbances to economic development and to strengthen the authority of the 'New Order' government. They have cast their shadow on all levels of government and taken many positions which should have been filled by civilians. To control the people, the Department of Defence and Security/*ABRI* [armed forces] has formed institutions and civil defence bodies all the way down to village level.[52] To justify their political role the military use the integral state theory. This was revived by Abdul Kadir Besar in his 'academic appraisal' contained in the 1972 *White Book of the MPRS* (the then Provisional *MPR*) Chairman. Later, in 1978 the *SESKOAD* (*Sekolah Staf Komando Angkatan Darat* or Army Staff and Command School), where Abdul Kadir was deputy commander, explained 'the implementation of *ABRI*'s dual function' in the context of the integral state theory, arguing that it legitimates the army's position as the central part of the 'family' *[Kekeluargaan]* of the nation.

In the 1945 Constitution, the military are mentioned as a functional group, in addition to youth, women, labour, religious scholars, intellectuals, artists, and so on. Then, after the launching of the programme of 'unity between *ABRI* and the people', in the 1980s, a new doctrine was formulated to the effect that *ABRI* would be committed not only to *Pancasila* and the 1945 Constitution, but also to the interests of the people. All this was an attempt to legitimize the armed forces' role in politics, seeking support from the theory of the integral state. So in practice and theory there has been a continuous effort to concentrate and strengthen the power of the 'New Order'. National political stability has been established as a guarantor of economic development, which has top priority - though in fact it benefits mainly those in power. In consequence, the nation has been moved even further away from constitutional government.

Firstly, human rights have been disregarded; this has been based on the argument that state and people constitute a unity, and government leaders automatically protect all the people - because they are united with them. As such, human rights are considered not to be in accordance with the integral state. However, the clear reality is that human rights have been violated throughout the 'New Order' period. For example, right up to the present people's land has continued to be confiscated for so-called development projects.

Several laws, for example that on political parties and *Golkar* (an acronym for *Golongan Karya* or Functional Group, the government party) clearly inhibit and limit civil rights. Indeed, democracy and human rights have long been considered too sensitive a topic to be discussed openly. It is only in the 1990s that it has become possible to do so.

Secondly, the 'family concept' (*konsep kekeluargaan*) has been cynically exploited. In terms of the relationship between state and people, the president is considered the people's wise father. This turns on its head the principle of popular sovereignty. If the people are truly sovereign, the president should not be the 'father', but rather the person entrusted by the people to lead, and who takes their aspirations into consideration. In daily life, the family metaphor is frequently used to cover up and repress conflicts which should be settled rationally, such as when people's land is seized for development projects. In these cases the important thing should not be whether land transfers are settled in a family atmosphere, but that land owners are given appropriate compensation. Another example of the application of the family principle, with its unrealistic assumptions regarding harmony and balance, is the relationship between workers and employers, known as *HIP* (*Hubungan Industrial Pancasila* or Pancasila Industrial Relations). A harmonious 'family' relationship would be possible here only if employers did not exploit workers, and if these felt part of the company, as sometimes in Japan. In fact, both sides have always been in conflict, and the government usually takes the side of the employer. The 'family principles' of Pancasila Industrial Relations really serve only to repress workers, in order that they do not demand their rights.

As mentioned above, the 'family principle' has also been used by the armed forces in the hope that they will be seen as an integral part of the whole 'national family', and so have their 'dual function' legitimized. David Jenkins, when discussing Abdul Kadir Besar's 1978 paper for SESKOAD, mentioned above, concluded:

> 'Indonesian cultural values are posited on the notion that every member of a family has a responsibility for the welfare of the whole family. From this flows the idea that an *ABRI* [armed forces] man is responsible not just for defence of the state but for developing, inter alia, its economic, cultural and political life ... *ABRI* as a member of a large Indonesian family whose particular duty is to defend the nation, may have a relative who, in implementing his duty in the economic, cultural, or political field, experiences difficulties or fails -- then *ABRI* has the right to, and is responsible for, assisting his troubled family member ... In the state based on family principles, a citizen who enters military service does not undergo a change in status; because of that, the principles of "civilian supremacy" and civil-military relations are unknown and invalid.'[53]

Thirdly, the theory of the integral state has been made identical with national integration and stability, so that it has long been forbidden to question it. To do so would be considered a threat not only to the nation's unity, integrity and stability but also, even more seriously, to the foundations of the sacrosanct 1945 Constitution. In this way, the establishment's power and the dual function of the armed forces are safeguarded forever.

Fourthly, an exaggerated stress on unity tends to submerge the principles of diversity, group interests and protection of the individual. It has weakened all pillars of democracy. This has been done by using loopholes in the 1945 Constitution. The principle of rule of law has been suppressed by legislation which has paralysed any notion of an independent judiciary. The elucidation of Articles 24 and 25 on judicial powers (the Supreme Court and other courts of law) of the 1945 Constitution states:

> 'Judicial powers shall be free, meaning free from the influence of government authority. In this connection, the position of judges shall be guaranteed by law.'

An independent judiciary is therefore clearly recognized. But both articles have been read and manipulated in such a way that the judiciary have been deprived of independence. Article 11 para 1 of Law number 14 of 1970 on 'The fundamental basis of judicial authority' states that the organization, administration (personnel) and finance of judicial institutions shall come under the authority of various departments. The public courts have therefore been placed under the Department of Justice; the religious courts under Religious Affairs; and the military courts under *Hankam* [Defense and Security]. In other words, judges have been made civil servants. The consequence is clear. For example, the Elucidation Article 13 para 1 of Law No. 2 of 1986 on the General Judiciary makes the Minister of Justice responsible for guidance and control of judges in the public courts - just as he is for civil servants. It is therefore difficult to avoid intervention by the executive in the functioning of the judiciary for the simple reason that administrative matters (position, career path) and finance (salaries and other facilities) affecting judges are determined by the department. Judges are also automatically obliged to become members of *Korpri* (the Civil Servants Corps) and are thus expected to maintain 'monoloyalty', with the duty to vote for the government's party, Golkar, in general elections.

The result is that law has increasingly lost its authority. Many judicial institutions are despized by the community. Court decisions can be manipulated and bought. It is impossible for any decisions to be made which might harm the government. Indeed many court decisions are settled behind the scenes by extra-judicial institutions like *Bakorstanas* (*Badan Koordinasi Stabilitas Nasional* or National Stability Coordination Board). This is part of the Department of Defence and Security, and is assigned the task of ensuring security and social order. These unconstitutional institutions have been very active in curbing social unrest and suppressing leaders and activities of whom government disapproved.

There are many legal provisions and laws in a whole range of fields which are in fundamental conflict with rule of law. Take, for example, Law No. 8 of 1985 on mass organizations. Article 2 (1), Article 3 and Articles 12 to 17 explicitly allow state intervention in mass organizations, in matters of principles, aims, and guidance, right through to their dissolution. The definition of mass organization under this law is any organization formed voluntarily by members of the community, who are citizens of Indonesia, on the basis of shared activity, profession, function, religion or belief in God. In fact such intervention should be prohibited, because it conflicts with their voluntary character. As Arendt[54] argues, any state authority which continuously attempts to control and dominate every institutionalized form of expression in the community is totalitarian. Totalitarianism aims at totally integrating all institutions which exist in the community into a single political pattern or framework. This political structure not only prohibits opposition, but also prevents community institutions becoming autonomous, beginning with the family, right through to economic institutions.

Law No. 21 of 1982 on 'Fundamental Provisions on the Press' is similar. Article 13 paragraphs 5 and 6 require newspaper publishers to possess a *SIUPP* (Press Publication and Business Permit) which can be arbitrarily cancelled at any time by the authorities without court proceedings. This law is in direct conflict with Article 28 of the 1945 Constitution regarding freedom of expression both in oral and written form.

The weakness of the position and role of the *DPR* is also reflected in legislation. Two political parties and Golkar emerged from the simplification in 1973 of the previous nine parties. According to the 'Law on Political Parties and Golkar', No. 3 of 1973 as amended in 1985, these three political organizations must be based on the sole principle of *Pancasila* and are under the guidance of the Minister of Internal Affairs. So, *PDI* and *PPP* are subordinated to and made part of the government structure, permitting the government to interfere at any time in their affairs; the party and its members are no longer independent. This never happened during Soekarno's 'Old Order'; parties and people, even outside the inner circles of the state, were then far more independent than at present. And, of course, the provisions which allow only the three political organizations are in contradiction with the basic right to organize, which is guaranteed in democratic countries throughout the world.

The position of the two political parties and Golkar is in any case ambiguous. What is the status of whichever of them wins a general election? Although Golkar has repeatedly done so, it has never become the ruling party. Instead it has remained the ruler's party, in other words, simply an instrument of government. In the final analysis, the three political parties are just tools in the competition between the real centres of power within the regime led by the president.

With its doctrine of the 'floating mass', Law No. 3 of 1975/85 forbids the organization of political parties and Golkar at the village level. It is thus a means of depoliticizing rural people and alienating them from political parties. This depoliticization also applies to the press, community (non-governmental) organizations, labour and cross - campus and intra-university student organizations. Popular aspirations may be channelled only through formal political institutions, namely the two political parties and Golkar in the first instance and the *DPR* in the second. However the *DPR*, bound by its own regulations and rules of procedure, can do nothing but follow the government's wishes.

Another striking fact is that the law on the 'Composition and position of the *MPR/DPR*', enables the president to appoint members of these legislative bodies. About 60 per cent of members of the *MPR*, formally the supreme source of authority, are appointed by the president; only 40 per cent are elected. In the *DPR* 100 places are allotted to the armed forces; only 400 are elected. This resulted from an agreement made between conservative parties and

Soeharto at the start of the 'New Order'.[55] In consequence, neither the *MPR* nor the *DPR* are independent, nor do they function as democratic representative institutions

Fifthly, as already mentioned, *Pancasila* has been transformed into an ideology which only the government can interpret. It has become a doctrine of the guiding principles of life within the whole community, nation and state. It is supposed to guide every citizen and state functionary as well as all state/community institutions. They are all indoctrinated by state-run *P4* (*Pedoman Penghayatan dan Pengamalan Pancasila* or Guidance Course for *Pancasila* Implementation) and refresher courses dominated by the integral state theory, with its stress on the unity and 'family' character of community, nation and state, over and above individual or group interests.

Sixthly, *pancasila* has been also made the sole ideological basis of all political and social organizations. This is identical with abolishing the identity of the different groups which exist in the society and contradicts the principle of *Bhinneka Tunggal Ika* (Unity in Diversity), which is the specific character of the Indonesian nation. In contrast, the late President Soekarno himself, as the architect of the 'Meeting for the Movement to Defend Pancasila', stated on 17 July, 1954 that *Pancasila* should be maintained as the basis of the state so that the nation would remain undivided. The *PNI* (the party to which he originally belonged) was based on its ideology of *marhaenism* (proletarian nationalism) but *PNI* would defend the *Pancasila*. But, he said, this should not be reversed: the *PNI* should not be based on *Pancasila*, because, if *Pancasila* became the ideology of one of the parties, then other parties would not be willing to accept it.

This kind of 'state idea' is known as organic statism in some Latin American countries. They have no guarantee of human rights, let alone democracy. The state through its repressive ideological apparatus holds a very tight and decisive rein. The people are organized into functional groups. This amounts to refusing to acknowledge the diversity in the aspirations and realities of society. Under the 'New Order' in Indonesia only one organization is recognized for each occupation: *KORPRI* (*Korps Pegawai Republik Indonesia* or Indonesian Civil Servants Corps), *HKTI* (*Himpunan Kerukunan Tani Indonesia* or Indonesian Farmers' Association), *KNPI* (*Komite Nasional Pemuda Indonesia* or Indonesian Youth Association), *Kadin* (*Kamar Dagang dan Industri* or Indonesian Chambers of Commerce), *PGRI* (*Persatuan Guru Republik Indonesia* or Indonesian Teachers' Association), *PWI* (*Persatuan Wartawan Indonesia* or Indonesian Journalists' Association), etc. Labour and farmers are the two social classes which are harmed the most because they are the lowest, especially in the rural areas. The middle class, such as entrepreneurs, managers, technocrats, technicians and professionals are free to obtain special rights;[56] they are leaders in the pursuit of the economic growth for which labour is sacrificed. Workers' rights are suppressed; labour unions formed by government simply become a means of suppressing unrest and strikes. On the other hand, lucrative business opportunities are provided to Chinese-Indonesian entrepreneurs. This is of course because by reason of their origins they cannot play a political role; if similar privileges were to be provided to indigenous Indonesians, they might be in a position to threaten the regime.

Thus, both the 'New Order', like the 'Old', has monopolized power and become totalitarian. Under both, *Pancasila* and the 1945 Constitution have been turned into an ideology to unite state and people under the president's leadership. Both regimes have given no room for the development of human rights or ideas of democracy. Both have been opposed to the principle of the limitation of powers and reject any idea of government accountability. And whilst countervailing powers managed to survive under the 'Old Order', under the 'New' they have been completely suppressed. So it is clear that both regimes, in power for a total of over 30 years, have been in no sense constitutional governments.

Prospects for constitutional government

The most negative impact of this repressive totalitarian regime has been the way it has obstructed the liberation of the people. During the 'Old Order' the people were mobilized, but they were aware of political interactions at the level of ruling elite, as well as of relations between ruling elite and society. They knew that all instruments of state and government and all socio-political organizations were directed to pursuing Soekarno's revolutionary aims. In contrast, under almost 30 years of the 'New Order', the political process has become completely elitist. All socio-political and social organizations are subordinated to the state, which exerts its authority over all social organizations, including traditional institutions in the villages. But the people are totally unaware of the struggles within the political elite and the various centres of power. Nevertheless, as was the case during the 'Old Order', all state, government, and political institutions affecting the lives of most people are engineered to strengthen the regime's power.

The participation of the masses in politics is limited. In spite of the general elections which are held routinely every five years, it is difficult to interpret the current system as democracy in any real sense.[57] The people are directed to support government programmes. Any act which is interpreted as not doing so may be branded as obstructing development. So workers' strikes or struggles against land seizures for development projects are frequently put down by force. Violations of fundamental rights occur frequently, even in the present day. They involve not only direct repression, but also sophisticated means, including limitations on the freedom of movement for certain prominent and vocal critics of the authorities, such as the 'Petition of 50'[58] members and others. Although recently such measures have become less obvious, they still continue.

Because such conditions have lasted for so long, the critical resources and independence of the community and its organizations have declined. The government, supported by the armed forces, has become completely dominant. As a result, only a few groups and community or political leaders have the courage to criticize openly the government's policy and actions. The principles of popular sovereignty, rule of law, and the division of powers, have not been able to function; they have been crippled by suppression and by legislation.

The question now arizes about the prospects for building a constitutional government in the 1990s. There are a number of reasons for hope. Firstly, constitutional or democratic government is not simply an idea once aspired by Mohammad Hatta, Sutan Sjahrir, Muhammad Yamin and other founding fathers of the state. It is an integral part of Indonesian history and is a basic commitment of the nation. Under 'Old Order' as well as 'New', the ideal of building a democratic system has remained alive. History has recorded that Soekarno's totalitarian regime came to an end because it conflicted with popular aspirations for democracy. Secondly, resistance to the totalitarianism of the 'New Order' has continually surfaced, even though it has been put down again and again by force. The resistance which re-emerged amongst student NGOs (non-governmental organizations) and other organizations during the 1980s has become more intense in the early 1990s and continues despite setbacks.

This indicates that the idea of building a constitutional government in line with popular aspirations continues to be a real factor in political life. A number of Indonesian NGOs such as *LBHI* (*Lembaga Bantuan Hukum Indonesia* or Legal Aid Foundation), *Fordem* (*Forum Demokrasi* or Democratic Forum), *Walhi* (*Wahana Lingkungan Hidup Indonesia* or Indonesian Environmental Forum), *Skephi* (*Sekretariat Kerjasama Pelestarian Hutan Indonesia* or Forestry Conservation groups), *Lembaga Pembela Hak-Hak Asasi Manusia* (Institute for the Defence of Human Rights), workers' solidarity forums, and student groups which have actively defended the people - and many others - have not remained quiet in the face of state tyranny. In the labour movement emerged a new independent labour union, *SBSI (Serikat Buruh Sejahtera Indonesia* or Indonesian Labour Walfare Union) to counter the corporate labour union *SPSI (Serikat Pekerja Seluruh Indonesia* or Indonesian Labour Union). After the banning of news-magazines *Tempo, Editor* and *Detik*, some journalists formed an independent journalists association, *AJI (Aliansi Jurnalis Independen* or Independent Journalists' Alliance) as a rival of the state controlled *PWI*.

Along with prominent figures both outside and within the government, and even pro-democracy retired armed forces officers, it is clear that the current democratization movement - although it is not yet solid - has a real potential for bringing about change. Now, in the middle of the nineties, it is apparent that the people no longer hide their disgust for arbitrary rule. The latest symptom of this opposition was the strong resistance to various government attempts to meddle in the political parties. Most branches of the *PDI* independently nominated Megawati Soekarnoputri (daughter of the late president) as their leader and opposed the government's candidates for their party. In the *NU* there is strong opposition against government attempts to replace Abdurrahman Wahid as leader by a more manageable candidate. And even in parliament voices critical of government are more frequently heard than in the 1980s.

I believe that at some point, all forms of pro-democratic resistance will coalesce and become so strong that they will force the government to democratize. However, two major problems are faced by the pro-democratic movement. The first is the definition of democracy. Discussion of constitutional democracy is bedevilled by the notion of 'indigenous Indonesian democracy' which continues to be strongly defended by Soeharto and his supporters. There is need to continue all efforts aimed at clarifying the implications of such ideas. The process of delegitimizing the theory of the integral state needs to be carried out by countering the doctrines, dogmas and thinking promoted through *Pancasila* guidance courses (*Penataran P4*) and other means. At the same time the notion of authentic democracy should be spread, taking into account actual characteristics of Indonesian people. Concepts of democratic state, popular sovereignty, rule of law and so on should be translated into practical terms. These are just as important as the political democratic movement itself, because without them there is the worrying possibility that we might return to the form of government we have had for the last 30 years. My study of the very important *konstituante* is meant as a contribution for the development of such ideas about constitutional government.[59]

The second problem is related to the strategy of the democracy movement. At the moment, this movement is neither united or integrated. There is real need for further efforts in this direction, by unifying and strengthening our vision and perceptions regarding democracy and democratization, and fostering our commitment to unity by formulating a detailed and reasonable common programme. We must also try to improve our organization and overcome divisions amongst ourselves. Efforts towards these three objectives: a clear vision, a policy for a programme of struggle, and better organization, should be made simultaneously. The obstacle to be faced is of course the power of the Soeharto government, been built up over the last 30 years into the strong and centralized system we see today, while the power of the people has been systematically weakened. It is necessary to rebuild it.

The role of the military, based on their doctrine of 'dual function', has been systematically maintained and remains dominant. They argue that 'dual function' will remain as long as the *Pancasila* political system is the basis of the state.[60] This doctrine is an obstacle to the development of democracy. It will remain the case unless and until the military are willing to re-formulate their role in the context of democracy. It may not be impossible that they - based on their commitment to the aspirations of people and nation - will in the end support and participate in the democratization process, as occurred in South Korea, the Philippines and Thailand. Verbally, some military leaders have begun to indicate such support. One staff member of the socio-political chief of *ABRI*, Brigadier General Roekmini Soedjono has declared: 'ABRI will continue encouraging democratic life based on *Pancasila* and the 1945 Constitution'.[61]

The possibility cannot be excluded that differences of opinion and interests within the ruling elite, including the armed forces, will emerge and that one or another group may obtain the support of a section of the pro-democracy movement. As identified by O'Donnell and Schmitter in their study of the transition to democracy in Latin America and South Europe, democratization does not always occur through violence, but usually emerges from a process of negotiation, where pro-democratic elements in the government structure were involved.[62] There is indeed no ready-for-use recipe for pro-democracy reform movements, but the patterns which emerged in these countries may be used for reference.

It would be wrong to see the state as the status quo party, and 'society' as pro-democratic. Rather there are pro-democracy elements in both society and government - even within the military - along with those groupings which support the *status quo*. Therefore it is necessary that the pro-democratic forces within and outside the governmental structure surmount prejudice and distrust of each other and work together. A widespread understanding of democracy, rule of law, and constitutional government is relevant here. If mutual understanding and trust increase, direct open democratic confrontation could be supportive for indirect, covert democratic influence. Especially if international pressure on Indonesia to democratize and to respect human rights continues, a change of attitude within the establishment is not impossible. The middle class which has emerged in urban areas, as a result of economic development, although so far tending to maintain an apolitical attitude may at some time also support democratization if not because of idealistic reasons than for practical ones. There is a very wide range of people who might support the democratic movement, which is now gaining strength amongst youth, intellectuals and the wider community.

If the democratic opposition grows ever stronger, the president and his government will at first certainly react with more blatant intervention, harassment and suppression. However, I note the global democratization process is continuing in South America, East Europe, South Africa, and South East Asia, despite temporary severe setbacks. So I believe that also in Indonesia the struggle for constitutional government, that is for freedom of Indonesian people within their own country, will continue and prevail over the totalitarian government.

References

1. The ideas in this article were developed from my thesis (Nasution, A.B. (1993). My appreciation to Paul Moedikdo Moeliono (Utrecht), Thohir Effendi and E. Shobirin Nadj for their comments and suggestions which assisted the development of the ideas for this article. I of course take full responsibility for its contents.
2. Lev, D.S. (1990).
3. Peters, A.A.G. & Koesriani, S. (1990), pp. 114ff.
4. Ilwain C.H. (1961), p. 146.
5. Greenberg, D. *et al.* (eds) (1993), p. xxxi.
6. Yamin, M. (1959), p. 65.
7. Feith, H. (1962).
8. The term 'Old Order' (*Orde Lama*) came from an army seminar in 1966 referring to Soekarno's Guided Democracy Regime (1959-1965); 'New Order' refers to the present Soeharto regime (1965 until now). Some critical intellectuals are now wondering whether Indonesia needs a new 'New Order'.
9. On various occasions I have reviewed the struggle between the concept of a democratic state and that of an *integralistik* or totalitarian integral state as formulated by Soepomo, professor of customary law, trained at the

University of Leiden in the Netherlands, who was a member of the Investigating Committee. I have felt it necessary to reveal the danger in the assumption which has been developed in the armed forces (*ABRI*) that the concept of the integral state inspired the 1945 constitution. This is clearly an attempt to legitimize the *status quo* and impede the development of democracy in Indonesia. See, among others, my paper (1993b).

10. The only source which records the debate at the Investigating Committee between, on the one hand, Soepomo's theory of the integral state and Soekarno's concept of mutual assistance and, on the other, Hatta and Yamin's democratic ideas, is Yamin (1959).

11. An ethnic group based in the province of West Sumatra. (ed).

12. For a good discussion on the political thought and obsession to unify the variegated Indonesian society, see Dahm, B. (1969), or Legge, J.D. (1972). Both the family concept as promoted by Soepomo, and Soekarno's thinking and actions were totalitarian. This became especially obvious in the latter's concept of 'Guided Democracy' which was put into practice between 1959 and 1965.

13. Yamin, M. (1959), p. 79.

14. Seputra, P. (1973), p. 316.

15. Yamin, M. (1959), pp. 299-300.

16. These articles of the 1945 Constitution read as follows:

Article 27: (1) Without any exception, all citizens shall have equal standing in law and government. (2) Every citizen shall have the right to work and to a living fit for human beings.

Article 30: (1) Every citizen shall have the right and the duty to participate in the defence of the state. (2) Conditions concerning defence shall be regulated by law.

Article 31: (1) Every citizen shall have the right to obtain an education. (2) The government shall establish and conduct a national educational system which shall be regulated by law.

Article 28: Freedom of association and assembly, and of expression in writing and the like, shall be regulated by statute.

Article 29: The state shall guarantee freedom to every resident to adhere to his respective religion and to perform his religious duties in conformity with that religion and that faith.

Article 34: Poor and destitute children shall be cared for by the state.

I share Marsilam Simanjuntak's opinion that Soepomo's concept of the integral state was basically rejected when the Investigating Committee accepted popular sovereignty as the basis or philosophy of the Republic of Indonesia, and included the basic fundamental rights of the Indonesian people in the constitution as described above. See Simanjuntak, M. (1994).

17. Seputra, P. (1973), p. 316; Dahm, B. (1987), p. 392. About Sukarno see also Legge, J. D. (1972).
18. (1949), The John Day Co., New York.
19. Sjahrir (1990), p. 285.
20. Seputra, *op. cit.*, p. 316.
21. Koesnodiprodjo (1951), pp. 50-59, 76; Sastrosatomo, S. in Anwar, R. (ed) (1980), pp. xxvii-xxxi.
22. Soedjatmoko in Sjahrir, *op. cit.*, p. 284.
23. Purwokusumo, S. (1951).
24. (1952),Department of Information, Republic of Indonesia.
25. See Pringgodigdo, A.K. (n.d.), and Sjahrir (1990), p. 281.
26. Sjahrir (1990), p. 281.
27. The 1945 Constitution may be amended, as specified by its Article 37. This requires that the *MPR* (the upper house) be attended by two thirds of its members, and that two thirds of those present vote in favour. At the meeting of the Investigating Committee on 18 August, 1945, Soekarno himself emphasized explicitly that the constitution was temporary: 'this is a lighting constitution'. He argued: 'When we have a state, we will be able to convene the People's Consultative Assembly which will draft a complete and more perfect constitution. (Yamin (1959), p. 410). But the present 'New Order' government has tabooed discussion of change to the 1945 Constitution.
28. Tan Malaka, one of the prominent figures in the revolution, who was both intelligent and popular, accumulated under his leadership about forty organizations, including the *Murba* (Trotskyist) Party, and the Indonesian National Army under the supreme commander, General Sudirman, in the *Persatuan Perjuangan* [Fighting Unit]. They challenged the Sjahrir government, especially with regard to its policy of resolving through negotiation the conflict with the Dutch. The *Persatuan* policy was known as the 'minimum programme' and demanded: negotiations on the basis of a complete recognition of independence; a government to be formed according to popular will; Japanese army to be disarmed; the problem of European prisoners to be resolved; and all foreign capital to be confiscated. Malaka, T. (1948).
29. Noer, D. (1987), p. 201.
30. Feith, H. (1962), p. xi.
31. See among others Feith, H. (1962), pp. 434-435; Seputra (1973), p. 370; Compton, B.R. (1993). pp. 272-273.
32. Compton, B.R. (1993), p. 283.
33. See, among others, Compton, B.R. (1993), pp. 392-415.
34. Seputra (1973), p. 381; Ricklefs, M.C. (1991), p. 378; Noer (1987), p. 265.
35. Compton, B.R., (1993), p. 11; Seputra (1973), p. 442.

36. Nasution, A.H. (1984), pp. 303-306; Ricklefs, M.C. (1991), p. 386. Nasution was the originator of the idea of *'dwi fungsi ABRI'* ['dual function armed forces']. He first presented it in 1958 as a *'jalan tengah'* ['middle way'] where the armed forces would be concerned not only with defence, but also with society and politics. (Lev, D.S. (1966), p. 192.) This paved the way for military domination of Indonesian politics over the last 35 years. Nasution himself has criticized the excessive implemention of his idea, but he cannot evade responsibility for it.

37. Noer (1987), p. 200, points out that there was a marked difference between the two types of cabinet of the 1950s. Working cabinets were either based on expertize, without considering party representation, or were formed to deal with special cases. The previous coalition cabinets had been based on the support of several parties, represented by ministers.

38. Feith, H. (1962).

39. Nasution, A.B. (1993).

40. (1956) *Risalah perundingan Konstituante* [Minutes of discussion of the Constituent Assembly], vol. I, pp. 25-26.

41. *Kementerian Penerangan* [Ministry of Information] (1959), *Kembali kepada UUD 1945* [Return to the 1945 Constitution], Jakarta, pp. 151-158.

42. Simorangkir, J.C.T., and Say, B.M.R. (1975), pp. 101-111.

43. Noer (1987), p. 256.

44. Seputra (1973), p. 397.

45. Nasution, A.H. (1981), p. 1.; (1984), pp. 303-306.

46. Notosusanto, N. (ed) (1985), p. 28.

47. Ricklefs (1991), p. 379; Seputra (1973), p. 379.

48. Soekarno (1961), p. 35.

49. Seputra (1973), p. 414.

50. Hazairin (1973), pp. 22-31.

51. Robinson, R. (1984), p. 35.

52. Hakim, A.G.N. *et al.* (1991), pp. 25-27.

53. Jenkin, D. (1984).

54. Arendt, H. (1960).

55. Notosusanto (1985), pp. 42-68.

56. Robinson (1984), pp. 35-36.

57. Ricklefs (1991), p. 428.

58. A critique of 'New Order' policies presented by 50 eminent personalities, including retired senior military officers. (Ed.)

59. A serious specific study on basic human rights, in addition to my own work on the Constituent Assembly, is that by Lubis, T.M. (1993). It is noteworthy that recently interest in this subject has been on the increase amongst lawyers, politicians, and others. The relation between human rights, democracy and constitutionalism, and how human rights are being

advocated in Indonesia, by *LBH* (Legal Aid Institute) among others, is discussed by Lev (1990), and Greenberg, D. 'Social movements, constitutionalism and human rights: comments on the Malaysian and Indonesian experiences' *in* Greenberg, D. *et al*. (eds) (1993), pp. 139-158.

60. Notosusanto, N. (ed) (1985), p. 368.
61. Soedjono, R. (1993).
62. O'Donnell,G., Schmitter, P.C. & Whitehead, L. (eds) (1986).

Administrative Guidance in Japan

HIROSHI ODA

Rule of law in Japan

Since the late 19th century, when Japan embarked on the course of modernization, Japan has had two constitutions. The first was adopted in 1889 in response to the 'popular rights movement' which demanded a democratic parliament and a constitution. However, it was prepared without consulting representatives of the public. The draft was never publicized. The constitution was simply 'granted' to the 'subjects' by the emperor.

The 1889 Constitution was modelled after the Prussian, and incorporated the principle of *Rechtsstaat* (constitutional state). However, unlike the concept of *'soziale Rechtstaat'* which was introduced in the German *Grundgestz* (basic law) after the second world war, *Rechtsstaat* at this time merely denoted rule by law rather than rule of law. There was a chapter entitled 'Rights and duties of the subjects' in the 1889 Constitution, but the rights contained in this short document were to be guaranteed within the limits of law, so that the legislature was free to limit them. Various laws enabled the police and public prosecutors to exercise broad power which led to the infringement of human rights in subsequent years. It would be useful to have a few examples here.

One of the peculiarities of the constitution, as compared to the Prussian, was the religious status of the emperor. He was characterized as 'sacrosanct' and was above the constitution. This arrangement of power eventually led to militarism in the 1930s and 1940s.

After the second world war, a new constitution was adopted in 1946 under Allied occupation. Unlike that of 1889, the 1946

Constitution is the 'supreme law of the nation'. All laws, ordinances, and imperial rescripts which are against it are void. A system of judicial review of U.S. type was introduced to ensure the supremacy of the constitution.   Whereas under the 1890 Constitution, the Imperial Diet merely assisted the emperor, who had the legislative power, under the 1946 Constitution the Diet is the 'highest organ of state power'. It should be added that universal suffrage was introduced as part of post-war reforms.[1]

The 1946 Constitution has an extensive list of fundamental rights. The list is not exhaustive; various rights came to be covered by the constitution through the development of case law. Since the end of the second world war, Japan has had a fairly good track record of protecting human rights. This is not to say that there are no exceptions. The treatment of criminal offenders at the investigation stage - restrictions on the right to communicate with the defence counsel, prolonged detention,   etc., - requires improvement. Discrimination against minorities such as resident Koreans is also a problem.[2] However, unlike some other countries discussed in the present symposium, in Japan there is no systematic infringement of human rights by government or military.

Rule of law is not only about the protection of human rights. It also includes democratic control over executive power. Rule of law requires executive power to be subject to legislation enacted by a democratically elected body which, in Japan, is the Diet.   The principle of 'administration based upon law' is firmly established in Japan. As mentioned above, the executive power conscientiously observes the law. However, whether the legislature exercises effective control over the administration is another matter. If the law allows the administration to exercise a broad discretionary power, this may erode the effectiveness of control by the representative body. In the following, the author would like to discuss this issue by focusing on administrative guidance.

The concept of administrative guidance

Administrative guidance has been, and still is, one of the favourite topics of foreign Japanologists. Presumably, this is because it seemingly represents the preponderance of 'unwritten rules' or 'informal rules' instead of formal statute laws in Japan. The underlying view is that while Japan has adopted a modern legal system based upon European and American systems, behind the facade there still remains the traditional system which is far from being legalistic.

However, in every legal system, there is a gap between statute laws and 'law in action'. Furthermore, in modern public administration, it is impossible to regulate everything by law; the administration has to be given some room for discretion to cope with various problems efficiently. In some areas, the legislature lacks technical expertise and the problem may be better solved if left to the administration. Therefore, it should be remembered that the problem which is about to be discussed is not necessarily unique to Japan. In fact, similar phenomena can be seen in countries such as Germany and the U.K.[3]

Guidance is an informal instrument utilized by administrative agencies (including local governments) in implementing their policies. Many people have attempted to give definition to administrative guidance.[4] One leading expert in this field has defined it as follows:

> 'Actions taken by administrative organs, although without binding force, that are intended to influence specific actions of other parties (feasance or non-feasance) in order to achieve an objective.'[5]

Administrative guidance is often classified into three groups; regulatory, reconciliatory and promotional/advisory, but they are not entirely exclusive. It takes various forms such as recommendation, advice, guidance, suggestion and encouragement/discouragement. Parties to which the guidance is addressed are normally private entities such as companies, trade associations and private persons.

Rather than discuss definitions in the abstract, it might be better to examine some examples.

Case 1

Due to the financial scandals of 1991 and the world wide fall in share prices, the Nikkei average declined from 40,000 points to 15,000 in two years. From 1992 to 1993 the Ministry of Finance, which is in charge of the stock market, resorted to what was later dubbed the 'Price Keeping Operation' (PKO). The ministry reportedly discouraged financial institutions from selling shares in the market in order to prevent further falls in prices.

Naturally, share prices should be determined by the market, but in some extreme situations, 'invisible hands' attempt to guide them. In this particular instance, the very fact that there was guidance was officially denied. However, it was reported in the press that financial institutions received calls from the ministry if they intended to sell a large amount of shares.[6] Representatives of major life insurance companies were summoned to the ministry and were asked to submit detailed reports concerning their fund management. Life insurance companies took the hint; the biggest soon afterwards invested 10 billion yen in the market.[7]

To be sure, there is no provision in law which enables the ministry to interfere with activities of financial institutions in such detail. However, in practice, financial institutions are subject to a meticulous control by the ministry and this case is merely an example.

As can be seen in Case 1, guidance is usually not based upon an explicit provision of law which enables ministers to resort to such action. Rather, it is often based upon the general supervisory powers of ministers. For example, in banking business, guidance is ultimately based on such powers of the Minister of Finance granted by the Banking Law. According to this, the minister may, if he deems it necessary to ensure a bank's sound and appropriate management, require the bank to submit reports or documents on its business activities or financial position. The minister is empowered to send officials to the bank, question its business activities and financial position, and inspect books of accounts and other documents. In extreme instances, he may suspend the business of the bank, dismiss any of its directors or auditors, or revoke its licence.[8] A similar power is available to him in various areas including insurance and securities businesses.

Although guidance does not have a specific statutory basis, it is often linked with the power of the agency to grant licences or permits. In the following example, guidance is linked to the power of the Ministry of Transportation to approve taxi fares.

Case 2

The taxi industry is supervised by the Ministry of Transportation. Taxi companies are licensed by the minister and fares are subject to ministerial approval. There is an informal rule that the fare should be the same for the same area regardless of the operator. In 1989, a consumption tax (VAT) of 3 per cent was introduced in Japan. Accordingly, taxi companies, under the auspices of the ministry, shifted the burden of tax to the users by raising fares. A taxi company in Osaka defied guidance and refused to apply for fare increases. The ministry encouraged this taxi company to keep pace with other companies, but failed to persuade it. In 1992 this company applied to the ministry for an increase of fare of 3 per cent. However, the ministry did not accept the application and, by way of guidance, attempted to persuade the company to increase the fare further, instead of a modest 3 per cent. The application was withheld for several months while the ministry was trying to persuade the company.

Guidance is informal in another sense. It takes various forms, including circulars issued by a vice minister or bureau directors. It is often given orally. Thus, in Case 1, guidance was partly effected by a phone call. There is no record, and the guidance itself is open to interpretation.

The most distinctive feature of guidance lies in its ostensibly voluntary nature; it is merely a suggestion or advice by agencies and, theoretically, it is up to the party to whom the guidance is addressed to comply with or to defy the guidance. However, voluntary compliance of the other party is expected and usually obtained. The implementation of guidance is often supported by potential disadvantages to those who defy it.

Case 3

In the aluminium industry, the Ministry of International Trade and Industry (MITI) has a supervisory power. In the late 1960s, when the market was in recession, the ministry planned to 'adjust' the number of electric furnaces and suggested that a certain number be closed. One major non-ferrous metal company refused. The ministry reduced its allocation of oil.

Case 4

MITI strictly controls imports of oil. A medium size company attempted to import it inexpensively. MITI tried to discourage this, but when it failed, through the Ministry of Finance, it put pressure on the bank which financed the company.[9]

Case 5

The city of Musashino has adopted guide-lines for residential developments. When a developer failed to comply with guidance based on these guide-lines, the city refused to supply water to the building, and prospective residents were therefore unable to move in.

Case 6

A real estate developer planned to build an apartment block in the city of Yokohama, which had introduced guide-lines for the development of residential areas. Based upon these guide-lines, by way of guidance, developers were required to contribute a fixed amount of money to a fund which was intended to support building educational institutions. The city refused to provide water and sewage service to developers who failed to follow the guidance.

Thus, guidance is not legally binding, but is often supported by the power of agencies which are responsible for regulating the industry.

Another feature of guidance is that it often strengthens the regulatory power of the administration. It frequently occurs that, by way of guidance, regulations set out by statutory law are further reinforced. As can be seen in the following example, although the law merely requires notification, in fact it is not accepted unless the applicant fulfils other conditions, not necessarily provided by law.

Case 7

In Japan, opening of large retail shops is regulated by law. This is intended to protect the interests of small retailers in the locality. The law requires that those who intend to open a large retail shop notify MITI or the local government, depending on the size of the proposed shop. However, in practice notification is not accepted straight away. In 'controlled areas' which MITI has designated, notification is suspended by virtue of guidance. In other areas, there is a 'prior consultation system' by which the consent of local retailers, chambers of commerce, etc., is required in advance of notification. An informal co-ordination committee is set up, and without the approval of this committee, the procedure cannot go ahead. It took nine years for one applicant to have the notification accepted.[10]

Availability of judicial remedies

As a corollary to the informality of guidance, availability of judicial remedies is rather limited. While acts (*verwaltungshandlung*) by agencies, i.e., prerogative acts, are subject to full judicial review under the Law on Administrative Litigation, guidance does not fall within this category. Therefore, it is impossible to contest the validity of guidance and demand its revocation.[11] On the other hand, it is possible to claim damages for illegal guidance.[12] Within such limits, the court has endeavoured to ensure its voluntary nature.

Thus, in Case 5, the developer sued the city for damages. The appellate court ruled that it was not illegal to suspend the consideration of application for the supply of water temporarily to enforce guidance. However, once the building is completed and residents are about to move in, it is against the law to refuse supply of water. Refusal is allowed only in on rare occasions where supplying water is against public order and morality. In this particular instance, no such grounds were found. This judgment was upheld by the Supreme Court.[13]

In Case 6, the developer was asked by the city to contribute approximately £100,000 to the fund. He tried to negotiate deferred payments and payment by instalments, but the city refused. He therefore had no choice but to accept the terms. When the building was completed, he sued the city and claimed that the contribution was forced on him, and therefore, null and void.

The Supreme Court ruled as follows:

> '1) asking a developer to contribute to the educational fund is in itself not against the law, insofar as the developer accepts it voluntarily.
>
> 2) the guide-lines in question were supposed to be an internal document of the city. Nevertheless, these guide-lines imposed obligations on developers, supported by sanctions such as termination of water supply. Furthermore, these guide-lines provided for procedures to ensure the compliance by developers. Moreover, the amount of the donation was determined by the city, and the wording of the document asking for donations could be interpreted to be compulsory in nature. Therefore, it is difficult to regard the donation as voluntary.
>
> 3) judging from the wording of the guide-lines and their implementation, the city was enforcing the guide-lines supported by sanctions which have been found to be against the law by previous judgments of the Supreme Court. Therefore, the city is found to have acted in excess of the permissible limits of guidance, and this act should be regarded as an illegal exercise of power.'[14]

Also, in Case 2, the taxi company sued the government for damages, i.e., the loss of income caused by the delay in considering the application for fare increases. The Supreme Court ruled that if the person to whom the guidance was addressed expressed a clear intention that he or she did not want to comply with it, the ministry should have proceeded and considered the company's application, instead of withholding it. Thus, the court found the ministry liable for changes.[15]

The positive features of administrative guidance

Guidance is a flexible instrument in the hands of the administration. It enables agencies to react to the changing environment and to cope with various problems efficiently. In the past, especially at the time of rapid economic growth in the 1960s, government agencies through their regulatory powers played a major role in leading the process and 'co-ordinating' industry. Ministries were seen as guardian angels promoting the industry they supervised. At times the government steered the industry through recession by allocating resources and co-ordinating production.[16]

In fact, the process of modernization which started in late 19th century Japan was led by government. Relations between government and industry have been particularly close. Government support and intervention are not regarded as necessarily evil, as in some other countries. Guidance has developed against this background.

In this context, it should be stressed that guidance is not necessarily a one-way process, i.e. a powerful ministry giving *de facto* instruction to private entities. Ministries and the industries under their supervision often co-operate in forming and implementing a policy.[17] There is constant communication and consultation. Indeed, it is probably impossible to enforce a policy without the co-operation of industry. Guidance does not come out of the blue.

It should be added that the legislative process is fairly slow. Sometimes, while waiting for the law to be enacted or amended, guidance fills the gap. An example is the introduction of controls over money laundering. The Japanese government signed the U.N. Treaty in 1989, but the law was adopted only after its ratification in 1991. In the meantime, a circular issued by the Director of the Banking Bureau at the Ministry of Finance 'encouraged' financial institutions to check the identity of customers and refrain from opening accounts under pseudonymous and anonymous accounts.[18]

Furthermore, there are instances where agencies as well as the opposite party prefer to solve problems without resort to formal procedures and opt for guidance. In advance of taking formal measures, agencies often issue a warning to the opposite party, and only when the latter does not listen proceed to take formal sanctions. This saves the cost of formal proceedings and also enables the opposite party to avoid adverse publicity. This approach was adopted by the Fair Trade Commission, which was in charge of implementing the Anti-Monopoly Law until recently.

Problems concerning administrative guidance

Although guidance is not against the law, there is a possibility that its widespread use may reduce legislative control over the administration. The interim report of the Provisional Council for the Promotion of the Reform of Public Administration, which was published in 1991, acknowledged the *raison d'être* of guidance. It enables the administration to react without delay to public needs, to achieve policy targets smoothly, and ensures flexibility of administration. However, at the same time, the report pointed out that over-reliance on guidance may result in the pre-emption of the rule of law.

In general, no specific statutory basis is required for guidance, primarily because it is not a prerogative act and not binding. However, if non-compliance of guidance entails sanctions, a statutory basis is required. General principles of law such as the requirement of proportionality and non-discrimination are applicable to guidance.[19] The outcome of the two litigations (Cases 5 and 6) supports this view.

However, if agencies can freely supplement regulations provided by statutory laws, this will certainly undermine the principle of legal supremacy, which is an essential element in the rule of law. Case 7 demonstrates the problem. In so far as the restrictions or conditions are accepted voluntarily, this is not thought to create a problem. However where, as in Case 6, the city added as a prerequisite to planning permission, without a statutory basis, mandatory conditions such as donations to public funds, guidance is illegal.

One of the negative features of guidance is the lack of transparency. Case 1 demonstrates the absence of records and the ambiguity concerning who is responsible for the guidance. Sometimes, this is nothing more than a tacit implication on the part of ministerial officials that allows various interpretation.

Case 8

In 1991, it came to light that Japanese securities companies had compensated their major customers for losses incurred on investments. At that time, promises of compensation were prohibited by the Securities and Exchange Law, but the compensation *per se* was not illegal. In October 1989, the Ministry of Finance (more specifically, the Director of the Securities Bureau) discouraged securities companies from opening discretionary accounts and advised them to close the existing accounts within a year. However, at the same time as the guidance was effected, share prices fell sharply (Black Monday!). It was impossible to close the accounts without incurring huge losses. Therefore, when securities companies were blamed for compensating losses - it is unfair to small investors and, in effect, distorts the fair formulation of prices in the market - some in the securities industry complained that they had merely followed guidance. The argument was that the ministry must have been aware that closing of accounts at that time would necessitate the compensation of losses, to which they virtually closed their eyes.[20]

Thus, guidance can be vague and allow different interpretations. Sometimes, even the very existence of guidance is denied by agencies (Cases 1 and 10). This illustrates the difficulty of contesting its legality. The availability of judicial remedies is already limited, since guidance is of a voluntary nature, but even where redress is available, it is difficult to prove the existence of the guidance or its contents, or to identify the person responsible.

It should be added that guidance presupposes a close co-operation between ministries and industry. In other words, it is based upon exclusive relations between the parties. Thus policies are formulated and implemented by a narrow circle of government agencies and industry. Since a specific statutory basis is not required for guidance, parliamentary control is insufficient. The general public is deprived of an opportunity to have access to information and to influence policy. Even within the industry, not all companies can take part in the policy-making process. In Case 3, while top companies within the industry cooperated with MITI, it was a company in the western part of Japan which defied the guidance, partly because it felt left out of the deal. In the securities business, it is well-known that it was the 'Big Four' companies (out of almost 200), particularly Nomura, which have influenced the policy of the Ministry of Finance. In some extreme instances, links between guidance and cartels were suspected.

Case 9

In 1974, the Fair Trade Commission recommended the dismantling of a price cartel formed by 12 oil sales companies. Directors of these companies were prosecuted for violation of the Anti-Monopoly Law. The defendants argued, *inter alia*, that the cartel was based upon guidance by MITI. Although there was no statutory basis to subject price increases to the approval of the ministry, prices of oil products were determined in accordance with its guidance. The Supreme Court ruled that this was legitimate, but rejected the argument that it formed the basis of the cartel.[21]

Growing awareness of the necessity for change

Although the significance of guidance as a soft, flexible, and efficient instrument available to the administration is acknowledged in Japan, the negative aspects of guidance have been recognized for some time. Already in the report of a committee under the auspices of the Agency of Public Administration published in 1983, the problem of guidance was addressed.[22]

Guidance was also an issue at the Structural Impediments Initiatives Talk, i.e., U.S. - Japan bilateral trade talks which began in 1989. The final report of the talks concluded as follows:

> 'In order to ensure comprehensive and government-wide transparency and fairness of administrative guidance, the government will ensure that it conforms with the intention of the Japanese Government that it does not restrict market access or undermine fair competition.[23] The Japanese government also undertook to implement administrative guidance in writing as much as possible, and to make it public.'

It is not surprising that guidance came to be focused in trade talks. After all, internationalization of the economy presupposes a system which is transparent and understandable from the outside. In so far as guidance is based upon a cosy relationship between government and Japanese industry, foreign companies will be at a disadvantage.

When the above-mentioned incidents involving the compensation of losses by securities companies came to light, the lack of transparency of guidance in relation to securities business was strongly criticized. As one of the measures to prevent recurrence of such incidents, the Ministry of Finance announced that some of the guidance in this area would be codified, i.e. incorporated in ministerial ordinances.[24]

In addition to the Structural Impediments Initiative talks, increasing pressure for deregulation has contributed to the changes. There is no doubt that government regulations have contributed to the orderly development of the economy. However, many have become inflexible and obsolete. Proponents of deregulation suggested that it will result in more business opportunities, bigger choice for consumers, and lower prices.

The governmental committee on economic reforms which has been discussing deregulation published an interim report in 1993. It referred to guidance and proposed that regulations be based upon statutes and that no regulations should be added to them. No disadvantages should follow from non-compliance of guidance, the content of which should be clear and transparent.[25] In a way deregulation reduces guidance, especially by abolishing regulations such as those of Case 7. It may also curtail the leverage of agencies to ensure compliance.

The new Law on Administrative Procedure

In 1993 the Law on Administrative Procedure was enacted.[26] Procedures to contest the validity of decisions by way of appeal and judicial review were institutionalized in the 1960s. However, a law to control the decision-making process of the administration has been lacking, though its necessity has been recognized for decades. Preliminary study of the law began in the early 1980s, but it was only in 1990 that the government moved decisively to enactment.

The law covers the process of review by agencies of applications for licences, etc., procedures for making decisions which are disadvantageous to the addressee, notification, and guidance. This last is defined as follows:

> 'Acts of agencies such as guidance, recommendation, advice etc. effected within their tasks or competence requiring specific persons to perform or not to perform certain actions in order to attain policy goals and which do not qualify as decisions (Art. 2, sec. 6).'

The law makes it clear that guidance should not exceed the task and competence of the agency. It has also confirmed that guidance is effected only with the voluntary co-operation of the opposite party (the person to whom the guidance is addressed). The law explicitly provides that those involved in effecting guidance should not treat the opposite party unfavourably because of non-compliance. For example, it is now prohibited to refuse access to information to those who failed to comply with guidance, nor may they be discriminated against in the granting of licenses and permits in areas unrelated to guidance.

When guidance is aimed at persuading the opposite party to withdraw an application or to change its contents, agencies shall not inhibit the exercise of the opposite party's rights by continuing guidance, provided the latter has indicated that there is no intention of complying with it (Article 33). Guidance should cease and the agency should proceed with consideration of the application. Thus, instances such as Case 2 above will not occur in the future.

The law is also intended to introduce transparency into the system of guidance. Thus, agencies are obliged to make known to the opposite party the content of guidance and the person responsible. Where guidance was effected orally, if the opposite party so requires, the agency shall issue a document which contains such information, unless this creates specific problems to the administration (Article 35).

If, in order to achieve the same policy goal, guidance is addressed to multiple entities, agencies shall determine its common content, and publish them unless this creates specific problems for the administration (Article 36). This is designed to introduce clear guide-lines and standards for effecting guidance.

The Singapore of what we might call 'the Lee Kuan Yew era' 959 to the present) has been to a large extent preordained by an ident of history which resulted in the failure of its federation thin Malaysia (1963-5). Much of what follows in this paper uld have been true even if federation had succeeded, but the sting out of Singapore into the unpredictable political vironment of 1960s South East Asia has resulted in the ognition by its leaders that Singapore is a potentially vulnerable y-state with a racial make-up which differs greatly from all the rounding countries. Indeed it was this racial difference, as well economic and political factors, which hastened Singapore's parture from Malaysia in 1965. The ideology put forward by Lee d other leaders since then has been that Singapore has only the elligence and discipline of its workforce, and no hinterland of e-padi and rich natural resources to fall back on, as Malaysia, ina and Indonesia have. Its only route to survival, let alone onomic prosperity, has therefore been to take advantage of its sition and infrastructure to provide goods and services to others, d to be a prime location for multi-national corporations. It is too all and vulnerable to withstand the shock-waves of a genuinely en society, and must maintain a rigid policy of social discipline d clearly defined, forcefully implemented, social objectives. This ge mentality is reinforced by, for example, the continuation of ional service and reservist training, even though there is no litary threat to Singapore. Attempts have also been made to enlist nfucianism as a guiding philosophy, but this has had limited ccess.

The ideology of social discipline has profoundly affected the velopment of law in Singapore. Law has been seen primarily as instrument of social engineering rather than as the expression of particular balance of principles defined politically or culturally d regarded as the embodiment of justice. This is a proposition ich would probably find few dissenters, but what I think is eresting is to speculate on the nature and extent of this analysis,

Concluding remarks

To repeat, in Japan there is little possibility of the government disregarding the law and violating human rights. The problem is the increasing power of the administration to the detriment of parliamentary control. The heavy reliance on guidance symbolizes the erosion of the rule of law and administration based on law. To be sure this is not unique to Japan; most industrialized countries face the same problem.

Guidance has played a major role in Japan's history. In fact, it was instrumental in the rapid development of the Japanese economy. However, with the internationalization of the latter, the disadvantages of guidance have come into prominence. Its ambiguity, uncertainty, and lack of transparency, are now being criticized. In addition, it is a reflection of an over-regulated system of public administration. Pressure for change has been mounting, and the new Law on Administrative Procedure has taken the first step towards reform.

It is premature to judge its effects. This is a general law which covers the entire procedure of decision-making. Specific reforms concerning guidance have to be made in each and every area of public administration, together with an extensive de-regulation. This is certainly an enormous task.

References

1. Oda, H. (1992), pp. 37-40.
2. See articles in *Law in Japan*, vol. 20, 1987.
3. For example, the system of bargaining in planning law in the U.K.
4. Haley, E.G.J.O. (1982), 'Gyosei-shioto and the Anti-Monopoly Law', *Law in Japan*, vol. 15, pp. 12ff.
5. Shiono, H. (1984), 'Administrative guidance' in Tuji, K.
6. *International Herald Tribune* (1993), 3 February.
7. *Asahi Daily*, (1993), 1 December.
8. Articles 24-27, Banking Law, as amended in 1993.

9. Shintou, M. (1992), pp. 123-124.
10. Nikkei (ed) (1980), pp. 69-76.
11. Article 3, *Law on administrative litigation* (law no. 139, 1962).
12. *Law on compensation by the government* (law no. 125, 1947).
13. Decision of the Supreme Court, 7 November, 1989; *Hanji* 1328-16.
14. Judgment of the Supreme Court, 18 February, 1993; *Minshu* 47-2-574.
15. Judgment of the Supreme Court.
16. Johnson, C. (1982), pp. 250-274.
17. Shinto, *supra* note 9, pp. 112-119.
18. Oda, H., and M. Yamane (1994), in Parlour (ed) pp. 109-121.
19. Shiono, H. (1994), pp. 169-172.
20. Oda, H. (ed) (1994).
21. Matsushita, M. (1993), pp. 145-147.
22. Government General Affairs Agency (ed) (1984).
23. MITI (ed) (1992).
24. *Financial Times* (1992), London, 10-11 August.
25. *Supra*, note 23.
26. Law no. 88, 1993.

'Smart' Laws in Singapor

ANDREW HARDING

Introduction

Ever since Sir Stamford Raffles in 1819 alighted at tl Singapore River where his statue now gazes benevo the backs of public buildings on the waterfront, Sing a byword for firm government. In his brief sojourn Raffles laid down many of the principles by whicl now governed: an economically ambitious policy of particular a free port; the recruitment of Singapore' communities behind government policies; law cleanliness; purposeful administration; centralizatic power. Raffles was motivated not only by utilitaria by humanitarianism. This latter aspect of his policy fulfilled, though only partially. Raffles would no dc with Singapore's prosperity and environment, the efficacy of its education, health care, public servi institutions, and its prominence in international would, I think, be disappointed that Singapore has r cultural focal point of maritime South East Asia, moved away from those principles of the enligh inspired its creator.

I mention Raffles rather than Lee Kuan introduction because it is easy to lose sight of Singapore's history, policy and legal system have be to a a large extent by geopolitics. It was chosen by l of its natural harbour, situated so as to serve India the West, China in the East, and South East Asia was from the beginning a commercial colony rather necessity.

and to see to what extent it represents a model for other societies to follow. Is law as social engineering in Singapore purely an outcome of its situation, or is it indeed a glimpse of the legal future of the 21st century, not just perhaps in Asia, but over the rest of the planet? To this question I will return.

Legal development in Singapore: common law and statute law

After the establishment of Raffles' colony, commerce brought with it Chinese, Indian and other immigrants from South East Asia and beyond. Commerce brings not only new ideas and values, carried by people freed from the traditional constraints of their own cultures, but also a motive for legal development: a degree of social stability and law and order is required; guarantees of private property and the honouring of promises; the legitimation and bolstering of institutions. The increase in population too, which in Singapore's case was an essential ingredient of prosperity, requires all these things.

Imperial policy required the introduction of the common law, achieved formally by Charter in 1826, and then by the progressive development of legal institutions - courts, judges, lawyers, local legislation, police, and eventually a bureaucracy, taxation, elections to a representative legislature, constitutional government, and political independence.

The most notable feature of Singapore's legal development during the Lee Kuan Yew era has been the growth of statute law. Of course this is probably true of every country in the world, but in Singapore it has taken a particular form. Statutes have on the whole conferred administrative powers going far beyond what is regarded in most common-law countries as appropriate or necessary, and to the extent that Singapore has developed an indigenous legal system with its own peculiar features, these features are almost exclusively uncommon in the extent to which they regulate social behaviour.

The legal system has become, in short, a regulatory system. In this one can contrast the emerging legal systems of other developing countries which, although occasionally embodying laws comparable with Singapore's, have been essentially pluralistic in nature, and attempt to establish a balance of interests, assuming a diverse rather than a monolithic society. It is this divergence of statute law from the standard model one generally finds in common-law countries which marks the autochthony of Singapore's legal system.

The common law, as is forcefully argued by Andrew Phang in a recent and very impressive monograph[1], has been characterized by its lack of development in Singapore. Taking the example of contract law, Phang shows how the judges failed to take a Singaporean view of the subject, simply applying English precedents mechanically, even where the needs of society demanded a different result. He refers to the 'emaciation of custom' and the lack of development of alternative forms of dispute resolution. Much the same can be said of tort law and many other areas of Singapore law. The common law is characterized by its failure to achieve autochthony, and, I would argue because of this, there is, in parallel, an atrophy of judicial power.

On this basis I want to take a brief look, by way of example, at some particular areas of public law in Singapore in order to amplify the thesis of this paper.

Constitutional development

Singapore inherited a Westminster-style constitution from its colonial past. After independence in 1965 a new constitution was promised, but in fact Singapore's constitutional development has proceeded by a series of amendments over the span of the Lee Kuan Yew era. Far from failing, like the common law, to achieve autochthony, Singapore's constitutional development has seen a series of experiments, and has probably now finally worn into its shoes with the election in 1993 of Singapore's first elected President, Ong Teng Cheong, under constitutional amendments passed in 1991.

Developments have centred around three issues, which are linked: race, opposition, and PAP succession. The objectives have been to recruit the support of the non-Chinese communities while suppressing communalism; to provide avenues for the expression of views opposed to those of the government without undermining the dominant-party system; and to ensure that the main tenets of Lee Kuan Yew's policy will be continued by his successors, and not be replaced by 'welfarism', which is regarded as the antithesis of PAP ideology, now that communism is no longer seen as a threat to Singapore.

a) Race

The racial tensions and riots of the 1950s and early 1960s made race an important issue after independence. A constitutional commission under the chief justice, reporting in 1966, was asked to explore ways of securing the confidence of the non-Chinese communities in their future as Singaporeans. The result was the Presidential Council for Minority Rights, set up in 1970, whose function was to scrutinize legislation to see if it discriminated against any racial or religious community. The experiment, promising in its original conception, foundered because the government insisted that members of political parties be allowed to sit on the council; the result was that the council was packed with senior members and former senior members of the government, including Lee himself as chairman. Naturally the council has never submitted an adverse report on any legislation; it quickly became an irrelevance.

The eventual resolution of the problem of ethnic minorities was the creation of the Group Representation Constituencies (GRCs) in

1988. The constitution now requires that certain constituencies, which supply one half of the total number of MPs, be represented by a team of three MPs elected as a 'slate' by the voters in three former constituencies now grouped together; one member of each slate must be a member of an ethnic minority, that is, usually a Singaporean of Malay/Muslim or Indian (South Asian) descent. Thus the voters may choose between a PAP slate and an opposition slate, but are bound to elect at least one non-Chinese MP, whichever way they vote.

The ostensible objective of the reform was to ensure that ethnic minorities were represented in Parliament. In fact the objectives were probably (i) to ensure that the PAP vote remained stable without resorting to the laying off of non-Chinese MPs, which would give the lie to the concept of a multi-racial Singapore; (ii) to make it more difficult for the opposition to secure an electoral victory in particular areas.

This would suggest that voters had not returned non-Chinese MPs in the past. In fact both the PAP and the opposition had included non-Chinese MPs, and some disquiet was occasioned by this reform, as it implied that non-Chinese candidates were unelectable. It is not insignificant that the visit of Israel's President to Singapore in 1986, which provoked an outraged response from Indonesia and Malaysia, was perceived to have provided evidence of disloyalty among Singapore Malay servicemen.

b) Opposition

The Singapore government has always taken the question of opposition seriously, even though it ruled in a one-party parliament from 1965 to 1980, and since then has been troubled by only one, then two, then four opposition members in a 81-member chamber. The reason for this is that, unlike most other countries, Singapore, as a city-state, has more or less identical constituencies; it is thus possible for almost total PAP domination of Parliament to be suddenly reversed (following perhaps some serious economic setback), into almost total defeat. Proportional representation was expressly rejected in 1966.

One solution, the creation of a one-party state, is closed off. Although the PAP has defined itself as a national movement (1983), it was forced by adverse reaction to concede that this was not a step towards elevation of the PAP to the 'leading role' given to communist parties in pre-1989 Europe. A severe reduction in the PAP vote at the ensuing election (1984) emphasized that Singapore, with a fairly solid 30-40 per cent opposition vote, could not go down that road. As a result, the PAP has had to countenance the legitimacy of parliamentary opposition, and has sought instead to control it.

The second option, the creation of non-constituency MPs, designed to give a seat in Parliament to the most successful of the unelected opposition candidates, an apparently generous gesture, did not solve the problem, as it proved unpopular among the opposition parties, who prefer to win their seats rather than rely on government charity; and the provisions, applying only where there are less than two opposition MPs, have been overtaken by events.

More recently, the creation of Nominated MPs (the third option), currently four in number, has met with greater success. These 'NMPs' can participate in debates and vote.

In case of PAP members deciding to cross the floor, an amendment introduced to deal with the politics of the turbulent 1960s ensures that they will not be able to do so without forfeiting their seats in Parliament. Indeed PAP MPs who vote against the government, or even abstain, are threatened with expulsion from the party.

Any notion that legal development has embraced political opposition, is however, quickly contradicted by the constant legal harassment of opposition MPs and the tough action taken against those who express opinions outside the arena of party politics. Not only the Singapore Law Society, but also NGOs and individual critics, have been targeted, especially in 'Operation Spectrum' in 1987, in which 29 people, mainly Church workers and social activists, were detained without trial under the Internal Security Act, accused of having mounted a Marxist conspiracy to overthrow the government. This action outraged international opinion. At present, however, there are no ostensibly political detainees in Singapore.

c) Succession

The notion of an elected presidency to replace the nomination of the president by parliament was conceived as a means of buttressing PAP rule, or at least the main tenets of PAP rule, and in particular as a means of preventing the dissipation of Singapore's substantial reserves. Although it was thought by most that this post was one into which Lee Kuan Yew would ease himself as he talked more and more of giving up executive power, in fact he remains as Senior Minister, and a former Deputy Prime Minister, Ong Teng Cheong, has been elected. His single opponent in the 1993 election was a little-known former civil servant.

The main problem with such an elected president is of course how his powers relate to those of the government itself. The structure created in Singapore is unique. The president is endowed not only with an electoral mandate, but with a formidable array of powers. He can withhold assent to certain bills, veto government loans, senior appointments and budgets of statutory boards and government companies, and exercise various other powers. In short, by use of his purely negative powers, he can bring government grinding to a standstill at any time.

Another problem with this reform, from the PAP point of view, was always that the presidential election might become a hustings for opposition candidates. This possibility has been preempted by imposing onerous requirements on presidential candidates, so that opposition politicans of the present echelon at least, are unable to stand. The rules are designed so that only members of the PAP-led political, administrative and business elite, can stand for election.

Concluding this part of the paper, I would observe that law as social engineering in the field of constitutional law in Singapore has been largely a success, judged in terms of the objectives of reforms. However, there is a kind of 'smartness' about these laws which could lead to their removal at some time in the future. By 'smartness', I mean that they appear to be programmed to produce not just in general, but rather too precisely, the result desired by their creators. This is a characteristic of many of Singapore's social engineering laws. They are the kind of laws which in the short term seek out their targets with relentless accuracy, negotiating every obstacle placed to thwart their efficacy; but in the long term they may be shorn of legitimacy by their very smartness - they are too smart for their own good. Perhaps they will disappear to the same part of the legal underworld which is reserved for Henry VIII's Star Chamber and the laws of the communist dictatorships of Eastern Europe. They do not provide a framework within which any future government, even perhaps a PAP government, would feel happy.

Administrative law and the administrative state

Administrative law has seen burgeoning growth in developing countries over the last decade or so, and we are now getting used to examples of judicial independence and administrative law reform cropping up in unlikely places, such as Indonesia and China.

As a generalization about administrative law in Singapore, I would say that it has displayed great activity but quite remarkable lack of development. The courts have proved very unwilling to question administrative decisions in most areas: compulsory purchase, taxation, citizenship, immigration, control of the press, to name but a few. By way of contrast, they have been willing to intervene with the decisions of tribunals and disciplinary bodies where natural justice has not been observed. But the cases have been few and rather insignificant.

As against the atrophy of judicial review and rule-of-law principles, administrative law in the narrower sense of regulatory statute law and meticulous enforcement has been developing rapidly. Hardly anything regarded by the government as a mischief has been left without drastic regulation: adverse comment by NGOs, lawyers, church leaders or foreign journalists; blocking of refuse chutes in apartment blocks; failure by the elite to perpetuate their genes; smoking in public; drug-trafficking; firearms; strikes; silent defendants; traffic jams in the city centre; crooked lawyers; traditional Malay villages (kampongs); official corruption; litter; chewing gum; and even unflushed public toilets.

In many of these things the Singapore government's actions have been amply and loudly justified. However, the smartness of the legal mechanisms used does not extend to preserving from collateral damage a large number of fundamental liberties. The statutes are not sufficiently smart to be programmed to distinguish between activities which are simply anti-social, and activities which may have a combination of desirable and undesirable aspects, or which may be wholly desirable. For example, restricting traffic in the centre at peak hours and the size of the car population in general seems sensible (to this observer at least), the infringement of personal liberty being marginal. The restrictions on criticism by the press, the churches, and NGOs, however, the sign of a healthy, democratic society, may (for all I know) marginally increase foreign investment, in the sense that Singapore will be perceived as a stable business environment, but the cost in terms of freedom of thought and expression, which any entrepreneurial society, let alone an open society, needs, is very great, unless one sees the population simply as an unintelligent resource, obedient automata, or 'digits', to use the word often used by Lee himself and other PAP leaders.

a) Habeas corpus

The development of habeas corpus is a good example of the smartness of Singapore laws. In Chang Suan Tze v Minister for Home Affairs the Court of Appeal had to address what is probably the single most important question of administrative law: to what extent can the courts review the exercise of a subjectively-framed discretion (in this case to detain persons under the Internal Security Act as a threat to security or public order)?

The court commented adversely on a previous decision denying the possibility of such review in security cases, and opined that the appropriate test was an objective one: the satisfaction of the president (acting on ministerial advice) had to be objectively reasonable, and it was not sufficient that the minister genuinely believed himself satisfied. However, the actual ratio of the case was that there was no actual evidence of presidential satisfaction. As a result, habeas corpus was granted and the detainees released. However, quite cynically, the government arranged for their rearrest outside the detention centre on freshly prepared documentation which complied with the court's ruling. If the court had framed the ratio of the case more generally, this would not have been possible.

Legislation was then passed restoring the previous law, excluding the relevance of the case-law of any other jurisdiction, and denying an appeal to the Privy Council in security cases.

The smartness of these laws goes even further. The appeal to the Privy Council could of course be abolished at any time, but has been retained because it encourages inward investment. However, the appeal requires agreement between the parties at any time before the case goes to the Singapore Court of Appeal, and is not allowed in security cases and cases involving professional discipline. Thus important commercial cases can still go to the Privy Council and be decided by British judges in London, but cases involving the government can be filtered out simply by the expedient of the government refusing to agree to the appeal, thus allowing the case to be determined finally by the Singaporean judiciary. The competence and independence of the judges need not be in issue: if their decisions are not sufficiently smart, they can be reversed by exercise of legislative power, and if this requires a constitutional amendment, the Constitution also ensures that the two thirds requisite majority is always forthcoming.

b) Eugenics

Another example which has become famous is the so-called 'Graduate Mothers Scheme', under which university-educated mothers were allowed certain privileges with regard to choice of primary school for their children. The object of this scheme was to encourage the reproduction of the elite, which was reckoned to have fallen behind that of less qualified parents. This represented the reversal of a family-planning policy which had been rigorously enforced by a series of carrot-and-stick methods over a period of several years, the object of which was to prevent a population explosion in a small island with little land to spare. The scheme failed, as very few mothers took up their rights under the scheme. After a vigorous defence of its purpose, the government quietly dropped it the year following its introduction.

What is interesting is that, although there was no constitutional challenge to the scheme, it was clearly perceived by a significant number of people as an illegitimate use of administrative power. Smartness, even in Singapore, has to extend to smartness about public opinion, even though the Singapore government has proved adept at opinion-formation, and has sometimes succeeded in altering what governments elsewhere might regard as an intractable environment of public opinion. The extremes to which government goes to alter the environmental of opinion makes the nature of Singaporean laws highly instrumental and regulatory, when taken in conjunction with administrative measures and campaigns.

Laws on voluntary sterilization and abortion have also played a large part in the eugenics policy; these have had the effect of encouraging and liberalizing access to sterilization and abortion, thereby restricting population growth.

To conclude this section, administrative law in Singapore has become law for administrators, not in my view a balance between the rights of citizens and the practical attainment of collective goals. There have been some very desirable consequences apart from the erosion of basic liberties: the virtual abolition of corruption, the provision of public housing and health care, and the reduction in environmental pollution, for example. None of these achievements can really be attributable to the denial of fundamental rights as such. Labour laws, on the other hand, have severely restricted rights of freedom of expression, assembly and association.

Conclusions

Let me now return to the question posed near the beginning of this paper: is law as social engineering in Singapore purely an outcome of its situation, or is it indeed a glimpse of the legal future of the 21st century in the Asia-Pacific region?

To answer this question one must gaze more widely at events in East and South East Asia, and look carefully at the crystal ball (or at the yam sticks!).

I hope to have shown how the development of Singapore law has been an outcome of its peculiar history, geography and politics. It would be an easily achieved answer to say that the case of Singapore affords us no general propositions about the future of state and law in the region or the world: it is a one-off case, albeit a remarkable one.

This would be superficial reductionism. There is much in the Singapore experience which matches that of the premier-league players, Japan, Hong Kong, Taiwan, and South Korea, and now also to some extent, in the first division, Malaysia, Thailand, China, and possibly also, looking to those aspirants for promotion, Indonesia, the Philippines, and Vietnam.

There is also no doubt that Lee Kuan Yew and other Singapore leaders see Singapore as a model for others to follow. This attitude is clearly shared by the leaders of some other countries. China has asked Singapore to create a Singapore clone at the city of Suzhou, near Shanghai. Thailand, Indonesia and Malaysia are co-operating with Singapore in the creation of special economic zones. Singaporean enterprises are investing in Vietnam and China; the latter has now become the largest recipient of Singaporean outward investment.

There are of course important differences. These countries all have autochthonous legal systems dating from pre-industrial times. Some are still communist states. Although they display different degrees of openness in their political systems, all have large and growing democracy movements, spawned by educational advances, the rise of a prosperous and ambitious middle class, and the influence of NGO movements and other international movements. In December 1991 President Ramos of the Philippines politely rebuked Lee Kuan Yew for suggesting a Singapore-model approach in that country, reminding him that his country had already tried an authoritarian approach without much success. It is a grave error, in my view, to think that state structures, political cultures and legal systems in Asia are similar or are converging.

The question therefore arises whether these emerging NICs, as they are often called, or newly democratizing countries (NDCs, as I would prefer) can pursue a Singapore-style legal system. I think the answer to this is that although, to an extent, they have already done so, further development of the region's legal systems along the lines of Singapore's is unlikely. Although it has been affected by the tail-end of the region's democratic reform-oriented movement, snuffed out in the 1987 detentions, Singapore has only marginally conceded a point or two to this movement, putting forward an alternative 'style' of PAP government under Prime Minister Goh Chok Tong since 1990.

The Singaporean educated middle-classes are a much more malleable entity than their equivalents elsewhere in the region, where important concessions have been made to 'multi-party democracy'. Even in Japan, the model which others in the region try to emulate, a coalition of non-LDP parties has taken power after two generations of LDP rule, an event unthinkable until recently. The effect of such events on Singapore has, so far, been slight. Even the present 'consensual style' of government has been able to embrace the dismissal of an opposition politician from his university post on the flimsiest of charges, and the hounding of Workers' Party leader JB Jeyaratnam resulted in some very adverse comments from the Privy Council. There is little sign that the new style is anything more than the old policy in new clothing. The necessities of Singapore's situation and the economic success achieved over the past two decades have enabled the PAP to immunize itself effectively against the democracy movement, albeit with some international disapproval. The size of Singapore has enabled a growth and effectiveness of the organs of state to an extent which even Japan, with all its social cohesion, has not been able to achieve. The severe anti-corruption laws protect the government from the most telling charge which is brought against its peers elsewhere in the region, and which fuels the demand for legal reform.

My conclusion is therefore that the monsoon-winds of change now sweeping the region cannot be broken by the wide espousal of a Singapore-type legal system. On the contrary, I think the question is whether Singapore itself will be swept along by these winds. My guess is that the legal system is now firmly entrenched, and that it will ride the storm. I envisage that much of the region will become, superficially, more like Singapore, but Singapore itself will have to make some concessions to the growing desire for rule-of-law institutions, or a *rechtstaat*, and the paraphernalia of constitutional democracy.

Reference

1. Phang Boon Leong, A. (1990), *The development of Singapore law: historical and socio-legal perspectives*, Butterworths, Singapore.

Human Rights in Thailand

VITIT MUNTARBHORN

> 'Last week one of our city's hapless traffic police officers finally could take it no more. Presumably succumbing to the relentless, inhuman stresses he had been meeting routinely on his job, the 25-year old traffic officer suddenly switched off all the lights at the Or Sor Mor Tor intersection to green and danced amidst the ensuing chaos. He was suspected of having a nervous breakdown and was taken to a mental hospital.' (*Bangkok Post*, 22 October 1993, p. 4)

This item from a leading newspaper in Thailand leaves the reader somewhat bemused. It highlights the horrendous traffic problem facing cosmopolitan Bangkok - like the weather in England, Thailand's everyday conversation piece. However, it exemplifies further some of the paradoxes facing the nation. While the country enjoys a growth rate of nearly 8 per cent per annum[1] and is advancing into the ranks of 'Newly Industrialised Countries', there is an underlying malaise concerning national development; not all is what it seems on the surface. At times, there is a sense of vibrant chaos behind the facade of normality, and this takes its maddening toll among the ordinary citizens of the land.

Likewise the rise of interest in law and human rights in the country.[2] Thailand's record on these matters often leaves the observer disheartened. Since Thailand's first constitution in 1932, there have been 15 others. Since the shift from absolute monarchy to constitutional in that same year, there have been twenty two coups, successful and otherwise, usually staged by members of the military.[3] After achieving power, they tend to overturn the existing constitution and to pass self-amnesty laws which exempt themselves from responsibility, even for the deaths and damage incurred by civilians during the coups. It is thus they who wield the hidden power of the land behind the democratic facade and the ever-changing constitution.

On another front, while the country is well endowed with a morass of laws and policies, implementation is often lacking - it is plagued by pervasive corruption. While there is a wealthy elite which can boast of several people among the top hundred of the world's wealthiest, there is a vast disparity between rich and poor.[4] While much of the wealth is concentrated in the hands of an urban elite, most of the people are rice farmers, many of whom remain deprived of an adequate standard of living. They are confronted with the trials and tribulations of uncertain rice prices and precarious land holdings in the face of ever-encroaching industrialization and environmental degradation.

In the march of history, what accounts for all these anomalies? Has Thailand managed, or not managed, to shake off the yoke of paternalism, authoritarianism and elitism in their multifarious forms? Although the country has had various golden occasions to promote a responsive legal system and a responsible statal machinery in this regard, there have been many missed opportunities. In several cases when these opportunities should not have been lost, they were - due to the vested interests which ultimately undermined other people's rights. Appropriately, a study of the human rights phenomenon provides us with key insights in this field; the struggle for justice and equity remains a constant and persistent challenge.

Origins

The roots of Thai (Siamese) law, ranging between the enlightened and the unenlightened, and the concomitant rise of the national state can be traced back several centuries.[5] During the Sukothai era (13th to 15th centuries), the more enlightened side of Thai law was displayed in the form of a stone inscription by King Ramkamhaeng which established various humane principles such as protection of injured enemy soldiers and asylum for those fleeing from catastrophes. Buddhist influences on human rights were already evident in these principles, and the role of the monarch epitomized a benevolent patron-client relationship. The monarch was seen as the society's fountain of justice and guarantor of human dignity. This was encapsulated in the stone inscription's immortal words that 'He who is troubled may ring the doorbell of the palace and the King shall come out to decide the case himself'.

That renaissance yielded to more troubled times during the Ayudhya period (14th to 18th centuries). The notion of absolute monarchy and the 'divine right' of kings, based upon Indian influences, gained the upper hand. The epoch coincided with many wars, and a decline in respect for human dignity. 'An eye for an eye, a tooth for a tooth' became the dominant spirit of the dealings between the people and their rulers, and the warring parties. Hindu law in the form of the Dharmasastra, intermingled with local customs, prevailed in the kingdom. The nascent legal system was closely linked with the monarch's own discretion and his brahmin priest - the Purohita - who administered the law.[6] The period also witnessed the advent of European powers in the region.

Ayudhya was superseded by the Rattanakosin era (the inception of the current Chakri dynasty) at the end of the 18th century, heralding the modern legal system of Thailand and consolidation of the Thai nation state. In 1805, King Rama I combined various laws of the land into the 'Laws of the three seals', a document on which were imprinted the official seals of the land. This was arguably the country's first legal code and emphasized the need for reform of the legal system, pressured increasingly by colonial conquest of neighbouring countries.

Sensibility towards law reform was heightened in part by the fact that the colonial powers brought with them the call for economic pluralism and more specific laws to protect their interests. The notion of 'extra-territoriality' was introduced in

1855 with the signing of the Bowring Treaty between Siam and the United Kingdom. According to this law, Siam allowed the British to establish their own courts on Siamese territory and exempted British subjects from the local courts. Other European countries followed suit. All in all, this meant that the Europeans regarded the local legal system as uncivilized.

The momentum for law reform was initiated in the reign of King Rama IV (1851-1868) and accelerated in the reign of King Rama V (1868-1910). Significantly during this reign, slavery was abolished. Rama V's extensive travels in Europe convinced him of the need to modernize the country, and he realized that some European institutions could be adapted for this process. It was also a matter of survival: modernization could make his country a stronger nation state that would have the wherewithal to resist external pressures and territorial encroachments. Law reform became an *instrument d'état* in this process. There thus began a series of legislative changes which would ultimately lead to the adoption of various codes based upon the Western model. The first instrument promulgated along these lines was the Criminal Code of 1908.

The reforms were continued during the reigns of King Rama VI (1910-25) and King Rama VII (1925-35). In 1932, the first *coup d'etat* was staged by opponents of absolute monarchy; the country was granted its first constitution and the age-old monarchy became constitutional. Would democracy or Prachathipathai be nurtured subsequently? As some commentators have noted:

> 'To Thais, Prachathipathai definitely does not mean popular sovereignty, control by elected representatives over the executive branch, power to the people. Political legitimacy here emanates down from the monarchy and bureaucracy to the common citizen, not up from the masses.'[7]

This was a missed opportunity. The 1932 coup was led by a Paris-trained elite, and did not really transfer power to the people. This top-down pattern would be repeated in subsequent coups.

In 1935, the Civil and Commercial Code was finalized, drawing heavily on the European continental system. Concurrently, there came into existence Criminal and Civil Procedure Codes. The groundwork for formal legal education and a national judicial structure was also laid during this period. On another front, extra-territoriality began to yield to national sovereignty; European jurisdiction on Thai territory was increasingly abolished. In the meantime, it was the military and bureaucratic elite which consolidated its control over the country, with questionable implications. During the second world war, General Phibun Songkram, a key military leader, led the country in acquiescing to Japanese influence. This nearly caused Thailand to lose her independence after the war. Ironically, while tactful diplomacy ultimately prevented this, thereafter Thailand would suffer from a particularly persistent internal malady: military rule.

The rise of Thai law and the nation state gave rise to some interesting queries which would ultimately have an impact on human rights. First, the legal system developed over the past few centuries was part and parcel of a statal machinery, particularly in the face of expanding colonialism in the region. It was and still is an essential means for consolidating the state and for 'integrating' its various subjects. What room would there be for pluralism, bearing upon the interests of non-Thais, minorities and indigenous peoples?

Second, particularly in the drafting of the various codes, European influence was highly visible, even though the country was never colonized. To what extent was it appropriate to impose the European model on the country? Were the Thai people, the majority of whom were and still are rural, ever consulted in the process? If not, did this merely sow the seeds for a top-down legal system without sufficient popular participation?

Third, the legal system that arose together with the Thai nation state was vertical by nature; it sought to centralize and 'uniformize' under an umbrella of statal echelons and hierarchies, represented by bureaucrats and administrators despatched from Bangkok to 'govern the rest'. In effect, this omitted the horizontal structures which had existed in rural and provincial areas from time immemorial, particularly the web of local rules and customs and the informal system of mediation and dispute resolution. How compatible would the vertical system and the horizontal structures be in the long run?

Fourth, the relationship between law and democracy, which would ultimately affect human rights in modern Thailand, was precarious from the start when there was a change of Government in 1932. As one observer commented:

> 'Not very long after the coup of..1932, ... the elite became uncomfortable with parliamentary politics; it had become apparent that democracy meant more than getting rid of the king. It meant public debate and frank confrontation. It meant questioning authority, and it caused frequent loss of face. By the end of the 1930s the Thai elite began to wonder whether there might not be better, less painful ways of obtaining the prosperity and power available to Western societies. Older and more authoritarian principles of leadership began to re-emerge. Demagogy replaced democracy as the Thai elite's new political panacea, and by the start of the 1950s the ideals of the Paris Promoters were all but forgotten.'[8]

These issues appropriately raise questions of democratization, pluralism, popular participation and access to laws and remedies, all of which are linked to human rights.

Human rights

Human rights can be translated into Thai as *sithi-manusyachon* or the rights of human beings. The word for 'rights', *sithi* made an earlier appearance in Thai history during the time of the absolute monarchy in the context of various laws concerning ownership; for example, a woman's right to matrimonial property and a slave woman's right to her child.[9] The word was used in regard to ownership in an inter-personal relationship rather than as advocacy of an entitlement against the State.

Interestingly, it is the word 'rights' rather than 'human rights' which has crept into the constitution. This is a fundamental distinction. While internationally 'human rights' covers civil, political, economic, social and cultural rights irrespective of racial or other origins, the word 'rights' in the Thai context has been used (at least in governmental circles) very much from the angle of rights of Thai people. This reveals a rather parochial and nationalist approach to the subject - this perception of 'rights' is of a lower standard than that propounded internationally.

This is exemplified by all 15 constitutions promulgated between 1932 and 1993. In the first, of 1932, there is one part which deals specifically with 'The rights and duties of the Siamese people'. Even in this context, only a limited number of rights were recognized, namely, equality before the law, religious freedom and a variety of rights on physical integrity, property, expression, advertisement, education, assembly, association and occupations. The notion of public order was also introduced to limit the enjoyment of rights. The duties enunciated included the duty to protect the country and to pay taxes.

Partly through Thailand becoming a signatory of the United Nations Charter (1945) and adopting the Universal Declaration of Human Rights (1948), the Thai constitution of 1949 had a more elaborate section on 'rights' as it was greatly influenced by the format of the Universal Declaration.[10] It replicated most of the provisions of the Universal Declaration, including equality before the law, freedom of religion, physical integrity, presumption of innocence, right to property, freedom of expression and association, and right to education. However, several rights enunciated by the Universal Declaration were omitted from that

Thai constitution; these included the right to privacy, the right to seek asylum, the right of freedom of thought and conscience, the right to social security, and cultural rights. Interestingly the rubric for incorporation of rights into the Thai constitution remained 'The Rights and Duties of the Thai People', and public order was again invoked as a pretext for limiting the rights recognized. This has been repeated in all subsequent constitutions.

In the meantime, new constitutions were introduced and abrogated with various *coups d'état*; from the 1940s to the mid-1970s, Thailand experienced almost continuous authoritarian rule. The provisions of the various constitutions of this period concerning 'rights' became merely lip service and a gloss for military-backed regimes. During this era also, notions of public order and national security were expanded extensively to curb the enjoyment of rights and freedoms.

The period coincided with the spread of Communism in neighbouring countries and Thailand's own pre-occupation with Communist sympathizers within the country. Various laws, such as the Prevention of Communist Activities Act 1952, were promulgated to confer broad discretion upon the state authorities to arrest and imprison people. The period also resulted in a government campaign against Communism to inculcate fear among the population and to justify limitations on political rights.

In October 1973, as a result of a student-led revolution, the governing military triumvirate was deposed and key military dictators left the country. What ensued was the constitution of 1974 - the most liberal to appear since the very first. It expanded the provisions of the 1949 constitution with such innovations as guaranteed political rights and equal rights for men and women. Yet only three years later, in 1976, there was another *coup d'état* which represented a backlash against the democratic movement, and the aspirations for democracy and human rights were suspended again for a while.

It was no surprise that the 1978 constitution which followed was weaker in its provisions on 'rights'. For example, the explicit reference in the 1974 constitution to equal rights between men and women was omitted, and although a majority of the provisions on 'rights' were repeated, the political structures for upholding the constitution were clearly different, as now the military ruled, albeit with civilian colleagues.

In 1988 national elections led to the return of civilian rule in Thailand. However, there followed many allegations of corruption against members of the elected government. In February 1991 the military, under the guise of a 'National Peace-Keeping Council', used these accusations as their main pretext for staging another *coup d'état*. They then established a civilian regime under Anand Panyarachun ('Anand I Government'). A temporary constitution was adopted in early 1991 and the final version was completed at the end of the year, superseding the 1978 constitution.[11]

The 1991 constitution is still in place today. Given the political circumstances facing its drafting, particularly the background of military influence, it would probably have been too unrealistic to expect it to be genuinely liberal or to be in conformity with international standards embodied in such instruments as the Universal Declaration of Human Rights - the committee that drafted it, after all, owed its origins to the junta. Nevertheless, the current constitution repeats many tenets of its predecessors and provides an insight into the perception of 'rights' in the Thai constitutional context.

Thus, there is a section which stipulates 'The rights and duties of the Thai people'. The rights include *inter alia* equality before the law, political rights in accordance with the law, religious freedom where this is not against public order, provision against retroactive penal legislation, the presumption of innocence in criminal law, the right to physical integrity, the right to property, freedom of expression and assembly except where limited by law, freedom of association in accordance with the law, freedom to establish political parties in accordance with the electoral law, and freedom of communication and travel except where limited by law.

The vibrant political chaos behind the constitutional framework would not be complete if one did not note that in March 1992, national elections were held, but due to the impasse concerning who should become prime minister, a leader of the coup of 1991, General Suchinda Kraprayoon, was appointed, even though not an elected member of parliament. He attained this position through a loophole in the constitution - it did not stipulate that the prime minister had to be elected.

This appointment led to massive demonstrations in April-May 1992. In May military detachments fired upon crowds of protesters in Bangkok; some 50 were killed, another 50 disappeared in mysterious circumstances, and scores were injured.[12] As a result, after intervention by the King, General Suchinda resigned after passing a self-amnesty decree. He was succeeded temporarily by Anand Panyarachun ('Anand II Government') who administered the country until new elections were held in September 1992. Significantly, before the elections a constitutional amendment was approved by Parliament whereby in future the prime minister had to be an elected member.[13] The amendment also managed to curb some of the powers of the unelected upper house, namely the senate. The September elections led to the return of civilian rule.

In this scenario, the following insights reflect on the meaning of human rights in the Thai arena as derived from the constitutional process represented currently by the 1991 constitution (as amended in 1992).

First, the reference to 'The rights and duties of the Thai people' reiterates the parochial approach to human rights; it provides for the rights of Thais, rather than those of all persons on Thai territory. It does not include those of minorities and indigenous peoples; it does not purport to be pluralistic. Ironically, for the protection of all persons, including non-Thais, one must look to the general criminal and civil codes and the procedural codes which do not distinguish between race and social origins. Unlike the constitution, these codes have not been overturned by *coups* and have in effect provided more enduring guarantees than has the constitution.

Second, the rights stated in the constitution are not absolute but qualified. Many are to be exercised in accordance with, or are subject, to law, namely they have to be implemented by other national laws (for example, an electoral law) or are limited by reason of law (for example, requirements of public order or national security). In addition, there is an umbrella provision which imposes an overall constraint on the exercise of all rights. By section 49 of the constitution, the rights stipulated cannot be exercised where they are detrimental to the state, the religion (namely Buddhism), the monarchy or the constitution.

Third, the rights stipulated are not justiciable in ordinary courts of law. These may not be used by Thais to question the validity of laws and policies by claiming that they violate the constitution. For this purpose, resort must be had to a special Constitutional Tribunal whose composition is closely associated with the executive branch of government. Rarely have individuals been successful in using this process. A key case in point to be mentioned below is the self-amnesty decree passed by the military-led regime in 1992, which was then tested before the Constitutional Tribunal.

Fourth, the reference to rights in the constitution is closely related to civil and political rights and freedoms, less so to economic, social and cultural, especially the right to an adequate standard of living and freedom from poverty, and the concerns of marginalized groups such as women, children, and rural people. References to the latter are not found in the 'rights' section but in the 'policies' section of the constitution. The key difference is that while rights are considered to be binding, policies are not. Therefore, while the 'policies' section talks of measures to raise the standard of living, the need to help the agricultural community acquire land, and the special concerns of women and young persons, these are not considered to be binding obligations on the part of the state; by section 59 of the constitution it is stated that policies do not give rise to any right to litigate against the state.

Fifth, the constitution reflects the traditional position that rights are constrained by duties. This often implies that the individual is subjected to the community and the family, and that individual rights are less of an imperative than communitarian interests. The current constitution has a key section on duties imposed on the people.[14] These include that of safeguarding the nation, religion, monarchy and constitutional democracy; conscription; payment of taxation; assistance to civil servants; and protection of the environment. In enlightened circles, a proper balance between rights and duties would no doubt be established. However, in the hands of the unenlightened, duties are likely to be interpreted as overriding rights.

In sum, it may be seen that the Thai constitution and its reference to 'rights' is not representative of a social contract between the state and its people. It is not genuinely based upon the universality of human rights as espoused by international instruments. It is more of an *instrument d'état*, representing the political undercurrents at play, and inevitably shaped by its *coup-prone* progenitors. It has more to do with the functions of government, for example, the relationship between parliament, the executive and the judiciary, in the context of the unspoken factor - the military - and less to do with rights and liberties conducive to accountability and responsibility on the part of the state. Any expectation of democratization, pluralism and popular participation as key expositions of human rights through the constitutional arena is likely to be met with disappointment.

To be fair, however, one must note that the governmental context is not the only one for deducing the meaning of human rights in Thailand. The past three decades have witnessed a significant increase in non-governmental organizations and a vocal press. Their perceptions of human rights are much more international in the sense that they tend to adopt universal standards and cite international instruments as an inspiration for their work. They are less parochial than their governmental counterparts in that they are willing to espouse the rights of non-Thais and a broad spectrum of marginalized groups. These tenets were illustrated in 1992 when Thai non-governmental organizations, together with other Asia-Pacific organizations, adopted the Bangkok Non-Governmental Organization (NGO) Declaration on Human Rights in preparation for the World Conference on Human Rights with the following reference to the universality of human rights:

> 'Universal human rights standards are rooted in many cultures. We affirm the basis of universality of human rights which afford protection to all of humanity, including special groups such as women, children, minorities and indigenous peoples, workers, refugees and displaced persons, the disabled and the elderly. While advocating cultural pluralism, those cultural practices which derogate from universally accepted human rights, including women's rights, must not be tolerated.
> As human rights are of universal concern and are universal in value, the advocacy of human rights cannot be considered to be an encroachment upon national sovereignty.'[15]

However, at the national level non-governmental organizations are still lambasted by conservative forces as being subversive. Nevertheless, the fact that it was the non-governmental sector that propelled the massive demonstrations leading to the demise of the military regime in 1992 attested to a universal message: the aspiration to democracy and human rights has no boundaries and cannot be classified as a purely internal affair. To wait for changes to be initiated by government alone in the long transition from authoritarianism to democracy is insufficient. It is popular participation which impels an accelerated process of change.

Civil and political issues

Whatever enunciation there is of civil and political rights in the national constitution, there remain many anomalies in Thai law and practice. Various situations give rise to a cause for concern. They may be broadly divided into the following: national security-related laws, *lèse majesté* (affront to the sovereign), freedom of expression and access to information, religious freedom, confiscation of assets, impunity of state authorities, judicial independence, and the criminal justice system.

a) National security-related laws

The notion of national security is influenced by the traditional perception of threats and the presence of an enemy - supposed or otherwise. The threat factor may be actual, potential or fictitious. This ambivalence gives rise to injustices precisely because national security-related laws are often used as a tool by authoritarian elements, who exaggerate the fictitious threat to consolidate their hold over the population.

The following listing of laws which derogate from civil and political rights in Thailand by reason of national security is given partly by Tongbai Tongpao, Thailand's most eminent human rights lawyer and a former political detainee:[16]

1. The Martial Law Act of 1914 which empowers military authorities to detain persons for interrogation for up to 7 days.

2. Prevention of Communist Activities Act 1952 which allows for preventive detention without trial for up to 480 days. Those charged are prosecuted in military courts and there is no right of appeal. Interestingly, the first law against Communism was passed in 1933 and provided this definition for justifying action against Communism: '"Communism" means economic methods or economic principles which aim at the abolition of all or part of private ownership of property by the state or collective ownership

of the people instead.'[17] The definition was expanded in 1976 by Order No.25 of the National Administrative Reform Council, i.e., the junta, to include the following: '"Communist organizations" means: -

a) Any group of persons or any party which aims to engage in communist activities, directly or otherwise.

b) The Communist Party of Thailand (CPT) or the various levels of the organizations of the CPT.

c) Organizations of the CPT which use other names.

d) The armed Communist terrorists...

"Communist activities" refer to the penetration, the propaganda, the instigation, the sabotage, the destruction, the coercion by force, or any other activities which aim:

a) to undermine the security of the nation, the monarchy or the democratic government,

b) to bring about a change in the national economic system, causing private property to be nationalised without any just compensation or

c) to reorganise a new social order based upon the principle of common ownership of property, except those organised as multi-purpose cooperatives according to the laws governing such matters.[18]

Over the years, a number of people have been arrested under this law. Given the fact that the world situation has changed radically since the days of the Cold War and that the CPT is now almost defunct, this kind of legislation is excessive and out of date.

3. Special powers of the prime minister to issue orders and decrees on matters of national security, permitted by various constitutions and special laws. These powers were particularly evident in the 1976 constitution and the various interim constitutions which have been part and parcel of the sum total of 15 constitutions, for example, the interim constitutions of 1959, 1972, 1977 and 1991.

One special law of note is the State of Emergency Act 1952 which empowers the prime minister and the minister of the interior to take special measures in times of emergency.[19] This was used during the May 1992 period by General Suchinda to issue orders prohibiting demonstrations by pro-democracy protesters. However, the orders were ignored. Another law used during this period was the Internal Peace-keeping Act 1976.[20] By this statute, the prime minister was empowered to appoint the supreme commander of the armed forces as the administrator of peace-keeping in the country. This law enabled the military-led administration in 1992 to monopolize decision-making with the help of military colleagues and to bypass the cabinet and parliamentary process in taking measures against pro-democracy demonstrators, with consequent unjustified use of force, and bloodshed. With the demise of that regime, this law was repealed in 1993 by the new democratically elected government, and a special force established for the Bangkok metropolis under that law has now been disbanded.[21]

b) Lèse majesté

Like other countries, Thailand has criminal and civil laws against defamation. However, there are special provisions concerning attacks on the monarchy, whether physical or verbal. For example, Section 112 states that 'whoever defames, insults or threatens the king, the queen, the heir apparent or the regent shall be punished with imprisonment not exceeding seven years'.

Over time, the lèse majesté provision has been used against various people. Locus standi (the right to intervene) is not limited to the monarchy; it is broad enough to cover those who feel that the monarchy has been harmed. This is particularly poignant as it may be used politically by some sectors of the community against others.

In this regard, it is noteworthy that there is currently before the courts the case of Sulak Sivalaksa, who has been accused of lèse majesté and of defaming General Suchinda.[22] He is alleged to have made statements at a public gathering detrimental to the monarchy and defamatory towards General Suchinda. Given the fact that the incident occurred in 1991 at a time when the junta was still in power, one may wonder whether the prosecution against Sulak is politically motivated.

Another incident took place in October 1993. The police director-general, Sawasdi Amornvivat, was dismissed by the minister of the interior, Chavalit Yongchaiyudh, for allegedly committing *lèse majesté*.[23] The circumstances are most intriguing. The police director-general had recently published in the *Royal Gazette* a ban on a Honolulu newspaper article which was alleged to contain words defamatory towards a senior member of the monarchy. Presumably inadvertently, the ban itself cited in published form the offensive words as used in the original newspaper article, thereby exposing the content of the latter to the public. Although the offending officer was granted a royal pardon, he was dismissed. In late October 1993, the story had not ended. In a newpaper headline of October 27, in another turn of events Chavalit was himself accused of *lèse majesté* as follows:

> 'Retired police officer Major General Supas Chiraphan yesterday accused Interior Minister Chavalit Yongchaiyudh of comments tantamount to *lèse majesté* by questioning former police chief General Sawasdi Amornvivat's right to seek a royal pardon.'

Police Major General Supas, an outspoken member of the Police Service Commission, said General Chavalit made the slip in the belief that Thailand was under communist rule and he was sitting in the Presidium.

General Chavalit told a press conference yesterday it was not right that the police chief had sought a royal pardon for alleged *lèse majesté* as the matter had still to be investigated.

Police Major General Supas said the remark itself constituted *lèse majesté* and made the interior minister liable to prosecution. He said anyone who heard General Chavalit's statement on the radio or television could lodge a complaint with the police.[24]

Whatever the truth of the matter, it would seem more logical that the complaint of *lèse majesté* should be limited to those immediately and directly affected, rather than that the community at large should have *locus standi*.

c) *Freedom of expression and access to information*

According to the 1991 constitution, Section 37:

> 'Every person shall enjoy the liberty of speech, writing, printing, publication and any other method of communication.'

This is, however, limited by law 'for the purpose of maintaining the security of the state ...'. By the same provision, the owner of a newspaper or other mass medium must be of Thai nationality. In addition, by Section 42 every person is recognized as having the liberty of communication by lawful means.

The general impression gauged from the operations of the newspapers in Thailand is that they enjoy a very free atmosphere. However, there are various laws on the books which have been or can be used to limit their freedom of expression. *Lèse majesté* has already been mentioned. Prior to the 1991 coup which overturned the civilian Government, the most infamous law restricting press freedom was Revolutionary Decree No. 42, enacted in 1976 during a dictatorial era.[25] The decree forbade the printing of anything defaming the monarchy or the Thai nation. Casting aspersions on the government and the promotion of communism were also considered offences. It obliged newspaper publishers to obtain a licence from the executive before publication. The punishments were severe - up to three years' imprisonment as well as destruction of publications. When the decree was promulgated, the executive had complete discretion to revoke newspaper licences without possibility of judicial review. However, by a subsequent amendment to the decree, the possibility of requesting ordinary courts to review that discretion was introduced.

One of the key achievements of the civilian government in 1990 was to abrogate Decree No. 42. However, other laws are still operational. There is, for instance, the 1941 Press Act which confers power upon the executive to control and suppress publications deemed to be contrary to the public interest, although in less restrictive terms than those imposed by Decree No. 42. There is also the Thai Criminal Code with its provisions on *lèse majesté* and defamation. Meanwhile, section 118 of the Criminal Code provides an all-embracing stipulation against comments likely to cause disturbances. These laws ensure that despite the generally vocal press, there are sporadic instances of censorship, especially by incoming coup-makers.

The situation is different with television and radio; they are state controlled. At best, some stations are licensed to private enterprises. The control of the electronic media by the state has been used by coup-makers and their allies to legitimize their origins through propaganda and to screen the news available. In the case of the May 1992 incidents, for a while the government of the day blacked out news of the shootings of civilians. The only alternative electronic news media were cable television and foreign radio. Newspapers were the relatively independent local sources of information, but the government tried to block this channel too. This suggests the need to privatize the electronic media and liberalize the information system as a whole, so as to ensure their independence, but efforts along this line have not yet borne fruit.

On another front, it should be noted that although there is generally the liberty to communicate, there is no guaranteed access to government information. Bureaucrats tend to stamp documents with the word 'secret' even when hardly necessary, thereby preventing public access. There is now pending the Official Information Bill which would ease access to state documents. It would 'guarantee the public's right to information, establish rules for disclosure, gathering and classification of official information, and protecting the privacy of citizens' individual data kept by the Government'.[26]   Interestingly, some official circles under the current democratically elected government have rejected the bill on the grounds of national security - a common, egregious official pretext for restricting the enjoyment of human rights.

d) Religious freedom

Section 27 of the 1991 constitution stipulates religious freedom as follows:

> 'Every person shall enjoy full liberty to profess a religion, a religious sect or creed, and to exercise a form of worship in accordance with his belief; provided that it is not contrary to his civic duties and to public order or good morals.
>
> In exercising the liberty referred to in paragraph one, every person is protected from any act of the state, which is derogatory to his rights or detrimental to his due benefits, on the grounds of professing a religion, a religious sect or creed, or of exercising a form of worship in accordance with his belief different from that of others.'

In other words, religious freedom is not an absolute right and can be constrained by reason of public order and morals. However, what constitutes the latter is not easily resolved; preferably it should be based upon reasonableness and proportionality.

In this context, there is pending before the courts a case concerning the Santi Asoke sect. As one observer has commented:

> 'Santi Asoke is the name of a Buddhist Temple or centre in Bangkok, having Phra Bodhirak as its founder.   Asoke congregations, who follow strictly the Lord Buddha's teachings, preached by Phra Bodhirak, are scattered all over Thailand. Santi Asoke and other Asoke congregations are officially separated from mainstream Buddhists and their Ecclesiastical Council since 1975.'[27]

The facts of the case have been described as follows:

> 'This Buddhist monk lawsuit is ... known as the Santi Asoke case. The two public authorities mainly concerned with this in Thailand are the Department of Religion, Ministry of Education and the Ecclesiastical Council. (For) the past ten years, these two institutions (have) considered the case to be the cause of disintegration and a threat to destroy Buddhism.
>
> The public prosecutor (has) accused Phra Bodhirak, the founder of Santi Asoke Buddhist Temple of "being a monk who regularly violates Buddhist discipline. The Ecclesiastical Council (has) decided (to order) him to leave the monkhood but he (has) not done so within 7 days of learning of the decision". For the moment, this specific case (has) resulted in becoming a criminal case in court.'[28]

The case is intriguing because it is generally accepted that there are various Buddhist sects to be found, e.g. Hinayana, Mahayana and Theravada, and there is generally no animosity towards them. Under the Buddhist Monks Act 1962 the Ecclesiastical Council in Thailand supervises the Dhammayuttika Nikaya and Maha Nikaya sects, but this statute does not forbid other sects. As the defence lawyer in the case has noted :

> 'Phra Bodhirak is not unorthodox. He is a Buddhist. He (tries) to practise Buddhist precepts according to his belief and understanding; a lot of people follow him. From what I see, his method is good and strict. He teaches people to be frugal, not to be superstitious, not to follow magic. He does not fabricate either male sex organs or sacred water. He does not perform black magic. He teaches people to work hard or to economise. Some of them even follow the Buddha's footsteps very closely, by eating once a day. What's wrong with all these practices?'[29]

Why then should there be hostility, particularly from the traditional Thai Buddhist hierarchy, towards the Santi Asoke group? Could it be because the sect is much more simple than the hierarchy in its approach to religion? Or could it be because the sect is seen by some sectors as having political affiliations with the Palang Dhamma political party, currently a member of the coalition Government? If there is this additional political nuance to the scenario, the case may be related to not only religious freedom and persecution but also political liberties and impediments.

e) Confiscation of assets

One of the first acts of the junta when it toppled the civilian government at the beginning of 1991 was the issue of a variety of decrees enabling it to administer the realm. By Decree No.26 of 25 February, 1991, it established a special committee to look into the acquisition of assets by politicians belonging to the previous government, with the power of confiscating illegal assets.[30] As a result, many assets belonging to a group of politicians were confiscated on the grounds that they were acquired illegally through corruption.

Granted that generally the confiscation of assets is dealt with in ordinary courts of law rather than by a special committee established by military decree, the validity of such an act *vis-à-vis* the politicians was questionable from the very start. The act of confiscation ultimately went against the tide of the new constitution which would be finalized before the end of the same year. By section 35 of that constitution, currently in force, the property right of a person is protected, although restrictions are possible 'in accordance with the law'. Moreover, by section 25, all persons are to enjoy equal protection under the law, and by section 29, an accused person is presumed to be innocent till proven guilty.

At first glance, therefore, the confiscation of assets by military decree was dubious in origin. When in 1992 there was a reversion to civilian rule after the September elections, one of the first problems facing the new government was whether to return assets to the parties concerned. The government hesitated for a while.

The Supreme Court, however, stepped in to invalidate the confiscation. The first of the politicians to win his case in court for the return of assets was Sanoh Thientong.[31] However, even then governmental authorities procrastinated by threatening to collect back taxes on the assets.

Nevertheless, the gesture of the Supreme Court was significant, especially as in the past it too had been timid towards the executive acts of military regimes. In the Sanoh case, however, it was forthright in its statement that Decree No. 26 had set up a special non-judicial committee to confiscate assets, an act which was against the democratic system and the constitution which had conferred the jurisdiction upon ordinary courts of law. The act of the junta was also tantamount to retroactive penal legislation, in breach of the affected party's rights, and the interim constitution of 1991 which was operational pending adoption of a new constitution at the end of that year could not be interpreted so as to confer the power of confiscation in this manner.

Two poignant lessons emerged from this experience. First, authoritarian regimes tend to manipulate local laws for their own ends in breach of human rights. Second, even when there is a return to democratic rule, there is no immediate guarantee that the elected government will undo the misdeeds of the authoritarian past, unless it is strongly pressed by other sectors of the community such as the judiciary.

f) Impunity of state authorities

The events of May 1992 are already well-known. In the midst of street demonstrations by pro-democracy protestors, soldiers fired upon the crowds and caused many deaths and injuries. A number of people also disappeared under suspicious circumstances, possibly murdered. An international report observed as follows:

'The use of lethal force by Thai security forces was unwarranted ... the security forces made no attempt to employ non-lethal methods of crowd control. There is strong evidence that security forces shot to kill, a deliberate policy that precluded less drastic action. In addition to summary executions, human rights violations included unnecessary and disproportionate use of lethal force, violations of medical neutrality and what may have been removal of bodies without proper inquest or autopsy procedures.'[32]

Would the military commanders responsible for the shooting be held responsible for their misdeeds?[33] The question was all the more relevant as a subsequent government inquiry revealed that the use of force against civilians had been excessive.

However, before General Suchinda resigned from the premiership in May 1992, he issued an amnesty decree for those involved in the incidents.[34] Although the decree covered street demonstrators as well as the soldiers, effectively it meant that those responsible for the misdeeds would not be accountable for their crimes but would remain immune from punishment.

When the newly elected civilian Government came to power at the end of 1992, the validity of the decree was tested in the new Parliament, and rejected.[35] However, there remained the issue of whether rejection of the decree would have retroactive efect so as to incriminate acts committed during the May period. The issue was sent to the Constitutional Tribunal for deliberation; it found that there would be no retroactive impact.[36] In other words, governmental authorities would not be empowered to take criminal action against the military for the offences committed in May 1992.

As a result, although civilians who wish to prosecute the military leaders in ordinary courts are not prevented from doing so, they are likely to meet with difficulties due to the findings of the Constitutional Tribunal which would influence judicial decision-making in any court of law. Whether those injured will try their luck in civil suits rather than criminal also remains to be seen. However, the whole scenario has left a strange aftertaste in the minds of those advocating accountability for military crimes committed against civilians. Even with a democratic government, there seems to be a sense of invulnerability vested in the military who have been deposed but who remain elusive while basking in their aura of impunity. It was another missed opportunity for nurturing accountability within a democratic system and another unjust derogation of human rights.

g) Independence of the judiciary

Judicial independence has long been part and parcel of the administration of the country. By section 190 of the 1991 constitution, 'judges are independent in the trial and adjudication of cases in accordance with the law'. Supervision of the judiciary is in the hands of the Judicial Commission in accordance with Section 193:

> 'Appointments and removals from office of judges of a Court of Justice must be approved by the Judicial Commission under the law on judicial service before they are tendered to the King.'

A furore was created by the interim Government under Anand Panyarachun (Anand II Government), which filled in the gap between the resignation of the Government of General Suchinda in May 1992 and the new elections in September 1992.[37] Shortly before the interim government's mandate ended in September, it passed a law to overhaul the Judicial Commission without sufficiently consulting the judiciary.[38] In its original form, the Judicial Commission had comprised 12 members: four ex officio members and eight elected from the judiciary. However, under the new law, the composition would be changed to 18, only six of whom would be elected by the judiciary. Effectively, the new arrangement would mean greater control by the executive branch of government.

This caused the most extensive demonstrations ever by lawyers and judges against the new decree. When the elected civilian government came to power after the September elections, the decree was rejected by Parliament, thereby confirming the original composition of the Judicial Commission.[39] Although this victory should not be seen as guaranteeing quality within the judicial service, it did nevertheless stem the tide of executive encroachment prior to the return to a democratically elected Government.

The painful lesson from this experience was that one needs eternal vigilance to protect rule of law and its basic component of judicial independence.

h) Criminal justice system

No analysis of the status of civil and political rights in the country would be complete without an appraisal of the criminal justice system, particularly its impact on the rights of the accused.[40] Despite the international exposition of the rights of the accused, access to courts and legal aid, equality before the law, and the presumption of innocence which are also found *mutatis mutandis* in the Thai constitution and the Criminal Procedure Code, there is much amiss.

The common sight of the accused arriving in chains in a criminal court sets the tone for analysing the shackles hampering the criminal process. First, a suspect or accused person who is poverty stricken will suffer more than a well-endowed person. This is most pertinent in regard to the granting of bail. Those unable to satisfy the pecuniary demands of bail are likely to languish in jail pending trial. Second, it is the police who are empowered to issue search and arrest warrants. This has enormous implications for abuse of power, especially if the police are badly paid and seek to manipulate the discretion conferred on them for their own ends.

Third, although the police are in principle allowed to detain a suspect for no more than 48 hours in ordinary circumstances, this can be stretched to seven days 'if necessary'. The latter again allows a degree of discretion which may lead to distortions. Fourth, although the accused has the right to a lawyer in court during trial in a variety of circumstances, no such right is guaranteed while the suspect is being detained for questioning by the police. Fifth, it is the police who undertake the questioning of suspects without the presence of other observers such as public prosecutors. This may result in malpractice and forced confessions.

These shortcomings have given rise to various debates concerning the role of the police and the need to empower lawyers and public prosecutors to intervene to protect suspects from abuse. So far, the police have not yielded to the suggestions aired below, and one can surmise that there are many vested interests at stake.

The solutions would seem obvious enough, if only the political will were there.[41] First, there is need to facilitate the possibility of bail for those of a lower economic stratum, perhaps through the establishment of a bail fund. Since problems of this kind often arise during weekends (with the prospect of a suspect languishing in jail from Friday to Monday), weekend facilities should be available. Second, the courts, not the police, should be empowered to issue search and arrest warrants. Third, police powers to detain a suspect for questioning should be limited to 24 hours, and if the police wish to detain the person longer, they should be compelled to approach public prosecutors to request a court of law to extend the period. Fourth, access to a lawyer should be ensured when a suspect is questioned by the police. The right to have a lawyer and the right to remain silent should be made clear to the suspect. Ideally, the interrogation should be videotaped to prevent abuses. Fifth, the intervention of third parties such as public prosecutors or others concerned should be maximized in cases which may lead to heavy penalties. In this manner, the role of public prosecutors, jointly with the police, in questioning the suspect in serious cases has been proposed as a means of ensuring checks and balances in the criminal process.

In the court proceedings themselves, the atmosphere should be to ensure that the basic principle of 'innocent till proven guilty' is strictly adhered to. Traditional notions of retribution and deterrence should be weighed with other concerns such as social rehabilitation and return to society. From this angle, fines and imprisonment are often antiquated means of sentencing inherent in the judicial process. There is much more room to explore an array of community service activities, particularly for less serious crimes. This should be coupled with a more proactive role on the part of the judge to scrutinize the background of the accused and to assess the chances of reintegration.

As an underlying philosophy, the trend should be to integrate the criminal law and process into the broader setting of constitutional rights and duties and international human rights standards. Yet, the long wait for law and policy reform in this regard may indicate another missed opportunity in the face of vested interests.

Institutions and personnel

From the various concerns raised above in the civil and political spheres, a variety of laws, policies and practices impacting upon human rights emerge at the local level - some good, several bad. Particularly for the ones that are more commendable, one is tempted to ask: how do law enforcement institutions and personnel contribute to their implementation? Conversely, for the ones that are detrimental to human rights, what are the remedies and what is the process of reform and change through the relevant channels?

a) Law enforcement

One of the key difficulties is the low quality of many law enforcement institutions and personnel, which has negative implications for the application of law and policy. The judiciary and the judicial system are cases in point. The formal judicial system is three-tiered. The courts of first instance are comprised of magistrates' courts (*kwang*) and provincial courts (*changwat*); they have mixed civil and criminal jurisdiction depending upon the seriousness of the case, the provincial courts enjoying broader jurisdiction. Bangkok has a more extensive system: district courts, Minburi Provincial Court, Thonburi civil and criminal courts, and Bangkok South civil and criminal courts. At the second tier is the Court of Appeal (*Uthorn*) and at the apex of the system is the Supreme Court (*Dika*). There is no jury system.

Strangely, in cases concerning conflicts between the constitution and other laws and policies, it is not the Supreme Court which is empowered to deliberate but the Constitutional Tribunal - an entity more aligned with the executive than with the judiciary.

The slow judicial process, backlog of cases, accumulated expense, and the need for expertise on specific issues has led to the establishment of special courts. The labour court and tax court were set up to overcome these difficulties and to enable appeals to 'leapfrog' to the Supreme Court without having to go through the Court of Appeal. The old system of juvenile courts with special judges to deal with child or youth cases was also revamped in 1991 to become the 'Youth and Family Courts'.[42] These special courts are innovative because they provide room for lay judges due to the desire for more expertise and popular participation. In the case of the labour court, a judge from the employer sector and a judge from the employee sector have to be appointed to sit with a traditional judge. Likewise, in the case of the youth and family courts, at least two persons well versed in child and family matters sit to hear cases together with two traditional judges; at least one of these must be a woman.

Yet, the official system is far removed from the rural people and other disadvantaged groups. There are no mobile courts to service the community. Disadvantaged people are also likely to find the judicial system expensive to use and dishearteningly slow, despite the availability of some legal aid. However, there have been attempts on the part of the executive to promote mediation committees drawn from village elders and paralegal personnel at the local level to provide alternative services. This has at times pitted the executive against the judiciary in terms of overlapping jurisdiction. A major obstacle facing the local mediation committees is that they may act too much in accordance with their discretion and too little in accordance with the national law.[43] This is exemplified by the difficulties faced by some of these committees when dealing with non-compoundable offences (for example, theft is a crime against the State and the thief has to be prosecuted irrespective of the affected party's willingness to drop the case). If they release the accused person upon request from the affected party, this goes against the grain of national law which calls for prosecution of the culprit.

On another front, there are no administrative courts for quick services to review administrative action. Attempts to set up such courts have not yet borne fruit.[44]

Perhaps the most important challenges facing the judicial system are in relation to the unwritten rules of the game. Many undercurrents are at play to undermine the aspirations of justice which should be embodied in the judiciary. A case in point is the hidden power of court clerks and non-judicial personnel of the court who control many of the papers and documents used in court. If their motivations are tainted, it is not impossible to envisage the wording of written documents being changed behind the scenes. If they have vested interests in a particular case, their unwritten *modus operandi* may have negative consequences for the administration of justice, granted that the price may be high for all parties.

On procedural matters, one should not underestimate the use of delaying and other tactics, particularly among lawyers in court, to undermine the position of litigants. 'The defendant is ill today. May I postpone the hearing until next month?' is not an uncommon method of procrastination used to stretch the proceedings to the limit and to dampen the enthusiasm of other litigants seeking quick and effective remedies. The situation is not helped by the fact that judicial hearings are held a month or more apart. There is as yet no method to ensure 'a day in court' when all will be said, done, and completed.

On another front, the police, military and related personnel are also in the forefront of law enforcement. They are not well paid - this may account for corruption among several sectors of them. They may also collude with various business interests who form part of the economic oligarchy; indeed, it is not surprising to find several uniformed persons sitting on the boards of large companies. A major weakness already noted above is that of impunity among these law enforcement personnel, especially in critical times when civilians are killed and injured.

b) Others

As implied by the earlier discussion, Thailand has long had a strong executive, when compared with parliament and the judiciary as the major arms of government. In the precarious history of Thai politics, the executive is, of course, represented rather often by *coup*-makers and their allies. Together with a centralized system, its powers are enormous and it is difficult to constrain unjustified use of such powers, while to use the ordinary courts system to impugn executive acts presents an uphill task. As already mentioned, the courts are slow and expensive for the ordinary person, and there are no administrative courts yet to accelerate the remedies. Nor is there an ombudsperson system to provide a monitoring mechanism and linkage with parliament. Interestingly, a proposal to insert the idea of ombudspersons in the drafting of the 1991 constitution fell by the wayside.

What of parliament as both an initiator and reformer of the law, and a provider of remedies? A major problem rests with the fact that the parliamentary path has proved to be an intermittent process during the past half century of Thailand's experiments with democracy. The fragmentation of political parties, and the frequent presence of a splintered coalition government, also implies much bargaining based upon personal interests rather than ideals. Quite a few members of parliament from various 'satanic parties' are still supportive of the members of the military responsible for the shootings of civilians in May 1992. Such is the apotheosis of political antics, or the nemesis of political ethics!

On a more positive front, in 1992 parliament set up a Parliamentary Committee on Justice and Human Rights. It has been instrumental in toeing a liberal line on various issues, including the rights of refugees, women and children, and the rights of those displaced by official dam projects. It has also received complaints from trade unions concerning the disappearance of their leader, from an official claiming abuse of power by the Attorney General, and from villagers against embezzlement by the business sector. However, the committee has only recommendatory powers, and it is not a full-time body; it does not meet every day but is interspersed between other parliamentary activities.

At the other end of the scale, there is the non-governmental sector which exerts pressure on government both in terms of preventing abuses, seeking remedies for abuses and calling for law and policy reform. However, its work is not always smooth. It is at times branded subversive and as a foreign agent receiving funding from abroad; this year one academic has been teaching military officials that non-governmental organizations are a threat to national security! It is also difficult for these organizations to national security! It is also difficult for these organizations to register as associations and foundations, since they would be screened by the police as a pre-condition for their registration, and they do not enjoy automatic tax exemption for their people-oriented activities.[45]

One is tempted to conclude that the traditional separation of powers and functions between parliament, the judiciary and the executive is not sufficient to guarantee responsiveness to human rights. On the one hand, one must be perspicacious about authoritarian undercurrents and their allies which infiltrate parliament, the judiciary and/or the executive. On the other hand, another option must be fostered as part of the checks-and-balances system necessary to prevent abuse of power by the statal machinery. It is the non-governmental sector, including the mass media, non-governmental organizations, community groupings and individual initiatives, through popular participation which must be the additional counterbalance against *mala fide* elements, in the quest for democracy, development and human rights.

c) Orientations

In retrospect, given the vicissitudes facing Thailand in the past decades, any analysis of the relationship between human rights, law and state is likely to be met with many anomalous challenges. While the country enjoys propitious signs of economic development, it is still hampered by the remains of authoritarianism, elitism, paternalism and parochialism enmeshed in nationalism. While there have been some successes in reforming laws, policies and practices in this regard, the remnants of inequity and iniquity impede the Thai advance towards a more enlightened society.

There is an urgent need to elevate Thailand's perception of and respect for human rights to international standards. This depends, in part, upon its accession to human rights treaties and other international instruments; as a corollary, national laws, policies and practices which are inconsistent with these norms need to be reformed and rectified. The local tendency to raise the status of 'exceptions', such as national security arguments, to become the rule and to distort 'duties' to override rights needs to be countered. In this respect, it is worth recalling the spirit of Article 29 (2) of the Universal Declaration of Human Rights which constrains such arguments by testing them against the parameters of what would be permissible in a democratic society as follows:

> 'In the exercise of his rights and freedoms, everyone shall be subject only to such limitations as are determined by law solely for the purpose of securing due recognition and respect for the rights and freedoms of others and of meeting the just requirements of morality, public order and the general welfare in a democratic society.'[46]

The evolution of human rights under such instruments as the International Covenant on Civil and Political Rights also indicates a variety of absolute rights, such as freedom from torture and slavery, from which there can be no derogation. Particularistic tendencies which seek to confer a degree of relativism upon these rights are unacceptable where they aim to lower international standards.

Even with a democratically elected government, the country is in dire need of the broader vistas of democratization, decentralization and pluralization. The vestiges of past authoritarian regimes have to be overcome by greater popular participation and mobilization. Cultural discrepancies embodied in discrimination in their various forms, whether by gender, race or other pretexts, have to be eliminated by an extensive socialization process - through community education coupled with incentives through law and policy - to change attitudes and protect the rights of those affected. Power and resources should be devolved to local, provincial areas so that people may take charge of their destinies more directly. The interests of marginalized groups, including non-Thais on Thai territory, must not be neglected. In this regard, pluralization indicates the need to cater to a plurality of groups on Thai territory whose rights call for respect, and the institutions and personnel to do so should not be monopolistic but pluralistic. There is an intrinsic link with not only the checks-and-balances required between statal entities such as parliament, the judiciary, the executive and the military but also the catalytic role of the non-governmental sector.

The current state of the law regrettably tends to be curative rather than preventive. It seeks to provide remedies for some of the ills of society, but this suffers from poor law enforcement and the blockage of vested interests. It should be targetted more to the preventive dimension of human rights and the promotion of laws and policies which can pre-empt problems rather than respond to them when it is too late. This has much to do with laws and policies which can prevent poverty, such as responsive social security laws, and which can prevent exploitation and other injustices, such as laws against child sexual exploitation. It is related to the need to use law as an instrument to satisfy people's basic needs, on the one hand, and to prevent criminal elements profiteering from the community, on the other hand. On the curative side, the need to hasten reform of those laws and policies which perpetuate injustices, such as the wide variety of revolutionary and military decrees still on the books, calls for accelerated re-appraisal. This goes hand in hand with the issue of accountability to overcome past impunity on the part of state officials. Both the preventive and curative strategies have to be set in an interdisciplinary context, and the allies of human rights should be drawn from as broad a range of disciplines as possible.

References

1. Bangkok Post (1992a), p. 12.
2. For general reading, see: Kosananand, C. (1985), Sobhakvichitr, K. (1980); Chamarik, S. (1988); Jamnarnwej, W. and Muntarbhorn, V. (eds) (1992). (All in Thai.)
3. The 22 coups and failed coups were as follows: 1932; 1932; 1933; 1933; 1935; 1938; 1947; 1948; 1948; 1948; 1949; 1951; 1951; 1954; 1957; 1958; 1971; 1976; 1977; 1977; 1981; 1985; 1991. In 1973 there was a student-led revolution, the only popular revolution, leading to temporary demise of the military.
4. United Nations Development Programme (1993), p. 170. For 1977-1989 32 per cent of the population were identified as in absolute poverty, and the Gini coefficient denoting the poverty gap for 1975-1988 was 0.47.
5. Kraivichien, T. (1967).
6. Bunnag, M. and Aakesson, P. (1990) 'The legal system of Thailand', in Redden and Schlueter, pp. 9A, 30, 13.
7. Morell, D. and Samudvanija, C. (1982), p. 25.
8. Wright, J. (1991), p. 312.
9. Kreangam, W. (1992), 'Rights and liberties according to the constitution', in Jamnarnwej and Muntarbhorn, note 2, pp. 28-44; 28.
10. *Ibid*, pp. 34-38.
11. Office of the Juridical Council (1992), *Constitution of the Kingdom of Thailand 1991*. Bangkok. (English translation). The 15 constitutions, including interims, in Thai history were promulgated in 1932, 1946, 1947, 1949, 1952, 1959, 1968, 1972, 1974, 1976, 1977, 1978, 1991, 1991.
12. Bangkok Post (1992b); *The Economist*, 23 May 1992, pp. 25-26.
13. Amendments to the constitution in 1992: *Royal Gazette*, Vol.109, Part 72, 30 June 1992, pp. 1-10; Vol.109, Part 95, 12 September 1992, pp. 1-3 (in Thai).
14. *Op. cit.*, note 11, pp. 1-3 (Chapter IV).
15. Asian Cultural Forum on Development (1993), pp. 198-210; 199 (Item 1).
16. Tongpao, T. (1980), 'Thailand' in Regional Council ... , pp. 26-29.
17. *Ibid.*, p. 28.
18. *Ibid.*, pp. 28-29.
19. *Royal Gazette*, vol. 69/278, part 16, 11 March 1952, pp. 147-151. An example of an executive order based on this statute, prohibiting demonstrations, is that issued by General Suchinda in May 1992; *Royal Gazette*, Vol.119, Part 59, 18 May 1992, p. 4 (in Thai).
20. Suvit-swasdi, S. 'Who really pulled the deadly trigger?', in Bangkok Post (1992b), pp. 24-26.
21. *Royal Gazette*, Vol. 110, Part 38, 31 March 1993, p. 1 (in Thai).

22. Amnesty International (1992), p. 251.
23. *Bangkok Post*, 26 October 1993, p. 1.
24. *Ibid.*, 27 October 1993, p.1.
25. Muntarbhorn, V., (1992) 'Pressing for press freedom in Thailand', in Tshisungu, J. (ed), pp. 33-39.
26. *Bangkok Post*, 28 October 1993, p. 3.
27. Poompanna, A. (1991), p. 7.
28. *Ibid*, p. 21.
29. *Ibid*, p. 35.
30. *Royal Gazette*, Vol. 108, Part 34 (26), 24 February 1991, p. 2 (in Thai).
31. Supreme Court Dika No. 913/2536, 26 March 1993 (in Thai).
32. Physicians for Human Rights and Asiawatch (1992), p. 1.
33. *Ibid*, appendix 3. Of particular relevance are the *Basic principles on the use of force and firearms by law enforcement officials 1990* adopted by the UN Congress on the Prevention of Crime and Treatment of Offenders. Article 4 states that 'Law enforcement officials, in carrying out their duty, shall, as far as possible, apply non-violent means before resorting to the use of force and firearms. They may use force and firearms only if other means remain ineffective'.
34. Human Rights Watch (1993), p. 190.
35. Tantikulanond, V. (1992), 'If the amnesty decree is rejected, what will happen?', *Siam Rath*, 11 November, p. 12 (in Thai).
36. *Matichon*, 10 November 1992, p. 1 (in Thai).
37. The problem began during the Anand I government when the executive branch tried to encroach upon the judiciary by meddling with judicial appointments. See further: Mahakun, V. (1992).
38. *Dulpaha - Journal of the Ministry of Justice*, Vol. 39 (3), May-June 1992, pp. 3-10 (in Thai.) The whole publication is devoted to the controversy.
39. *Op. cit.*, note 42.
40. Nanakorn, Kanit (1992), pp. 19-22.
41. Muntarbhorn, V. (1992), pp. 19-22.
42. 'Act to establish youth and family courts and procedure in youth and family cases.' *Royal Gazette*, vol. 108, part 203, 22 November 1991, pp. 1-67.
43. *Op. cit.*, note 49, pp. 17-18; Muntarbhorn, V. 'Prospects and trends of mediation as an alternative to dispute resolution in Thailand' *in* Pe, C. *et al.* (eds), (1988) pp. 393-422.
44. The Juridical Council, a governmental entity involved with legislative drafting and law reform, has at times been suggested as an institution which can be converted into an administrative court. However, there should be a broad range of courts to expedite matters and provide expertise.

45. Muntarbhorn, V. (1991), 'Occidental philosophy, oriental philology: law and organised private philanthropy in Thailand' in B. Baron (ed), pp. 140-156.

46. *Op. cit.*, note 16, pp. 1-7.

Conclusion: Conditions for Rule of Law

LESLIE PALMIER

In the five states discussed above, rule of law, that is to say not only separation of judiciary from executive, but primacy of the former, has been unambiguously the case only in Japan. Even there, arbitrary rule has left strong vestiges, the so-called 'administrative guidance'. This is not illegal, being based on the general supervisory powers of ministers. But the result is, to give one example from Hiroshi Oda's analysis, that although

> 'there is no provision in law which enables the Ministry [of Finance] to interfere with activities of financial institutions in ... detail ... in practice, financial institutions are subject to a meticulous control by the Ministry ... '.

At the other extreme from Japan we must place China, where it is certainly not possible to speak of rule of law, and not even of rule by law. It is clear from Philip Baker's account that the country's rulers, namely the Communist Party, regard such rules as simply Western 'bourgeois' conventions which limit their freedom of action; arbitrary government, which recognizes no restraint, is usual. However, it must be emphasized that this is no descent from grace; China has never known rule of law. Perhaps the most that can be hoped for in the foreseeable future is rule by law, where the party, having announced a rule, does not change it capriciously. (Though without rule of law it is difficult to see how the party and state can be restrained.)

Very close to China in this respect, in fact if not in form, is Indonesia. As Adnan Buyung Nasution shows, the leaders of the nationalist revolt against Dutch colonial rule in 1945 were not minded to adopt the Western convention of limited government which, as mentioned in the introduction, they themselves had not experienced. They drew up a highly centralized constitution, with great powers in the president's hands. The leading theorist used a convoluted 'family' argument to the effect that government should not be subject to challenge by subjects. This proposition was rejected, and the constitution abandoned in favour of one which placed emphasis on rule of law, and responsibility of government to citizens. The events which Buyung Nasution describes led not only to a return to the original constitution, but to its subversion by legislation, in particular that which turned the judiciary into civil servants.

In Singapore, Andrew Harding shows that government fashions and refashions the laws on the one hand to protect itself from all challenge, and on the other to control in considerable detail the behaviour of its citizens. Thus, when the grant of *habeas corpus* by the courts released a detainee, he was simply re-arrested on amended documents, after which the government passed legislation to prevent any similar appeal in future.

This manipulation was possible because rule of law had been abandoned. Judges are no longer independent; they have been put on temporary contracts and the power of their appointment placed in the hands of the prime minister.[1] Then, in addition to maintaining the Internal Security Act, under which some were detained without trial for 22 years, Singapore also adopted a Criminal Law (Temporary Provisions) Act, where those 'suspected of criminal activity' can be detained, again without trial; several have suffered this fate for up to 12 years, simply on suspicion.[2]

Thailand is of particular interest as being one of the few Asian governments which has never had a Western legal system forced on it, but instead has evolved its own, borrowing where it would. Though its judiciary remains independent, the legally manipulated impunity of the army for its periodic coups makes clear that it is exempt from rule of law. The only restraint appears to lie with the king who, though strictly a constitutional monarch, has recently intervened to curb the military.

In attempting to explain the presence or absence of rule of law, it is probably safe to assume that all governments would prefer the convenience of arbitrary rule, and abjure it only when compelled. This was dramatically illustrated in one of the earliest recorded demands for rule of law, namely the *Magna Carta* of 1215.[3] In form, it was granted by the English King John to his barons. In fact, they had brought their forces ready to make war if he had not acceded to their demands.[4] One may be sure that if he had enjoyed a supremacy of force, matters would have turned out otherwise.

The balance of resources between state and subjects perhaps helps to explain not only why rule of law in Asia, where it exists, was originally imposed by a foreign power, but also its fate after the former colony achieved independence. The withdrawal or weakening of Western influence does not necessarily mean that traditional concepts of government become predominant and oust rule of law. In India for example, where the state depends heavily on the taxation of private business, among which are some very large industrial empires, the traditionalist Hindu *Bharatiya Janata Party*, 'whose purpose is to reassert the Indian, more specifically the Hindu, tradition', nevertheless accepts rule of law.[5] Introduced to the Philippines by the United States, it has long survived their departure, and has re-emerged after the country's subsequent severe trials. The answer may perhaps lie in the fact that neither of these states is self-sufficient, but requires financial support from its taxpayers, particularly the more substantial. To put it another way, the latter are in a position to inflict sanctions on the state. That rule of law applies is no accident; it is an expression of an implicit contract between the state and the rich and powerful entities and individuals who provide its resources. The arrangement also benefits, of course, those who are neither rich nor powerful.

China's totalitarian government has complete control over the economy, and is beholden to no substantial bodies for its resources.

It is therefore hardly surprising that rule of law is unknown; indeed completely anathema.

However, perhaps the most instructive historical experience is the Indonesian. As mentioned in the introduction, in the pre-war Dutch colony, rule of law applied to Europeans, but not to Indonesians. Quite apart from the fact that since Netherlands citizens enjoyed rule of law in their home country, they could hardly be denied it in the colony, it was the Europeans, particularly the large undertakings, who provided funds to maintain the colony's government. On the other hand, it was government money which flowed out to Indonesians, among whom the educated, as government employees, depended entirely on the state for their subsistence. In independent Indonesia, as Buyung Nasution makes clear, the first president, Soekarno, was ever devoted to the authoritarianism of the 1945 constitution. He was compelled to abandon it in favour of parliamentary supremacy only because student guerrillas, the most dynamic of the revolutionary groups supporting both him and the embryonic state of 1945, were in no mood to accept authoritarianism.[6]

Twelve years later, in 1957, we find the democratic system discredited for failing to meet popular exaggerated expectations. Furthermore, owing to an inability to raise sufficient taxes or to trim its financial obligations, the government had been unable to pay many state servants, including, especially, several military units. These had therefore gone into business on their own account, and had then progressed to declaring themselves independent of the capital.

All this gave a new lease of life to Soekarno's authoritarian ideas. What made them practicable, however, was the seizure in December 1957 by labour unions, apparently under presidential instigation[7], of all large Dutch firms in the country. The government of the day decreed that it was to control the firms taken over. However, a week later the army chief of staff A. H. Nasution, as autocratic as Soekarno, decreed that they would pass into military hands. By so doing, the army gained the pass; it had acquired great resources, which included oilfields. In principle, Soekarno as supreme commander could have ordered the army back to barracks and instructed the state civil service, among whom he had many supporters, to administer the seized undertakings. But this would have split the army, and civil servants would have found themselves facing army sergeants not noted for their gentleness. In any case, both army and Soekarno now had no need to seek the consent of the governed. When the recently elected Constituent Assembly, discussed above by Buyung Nasution, refused to endorse Soekarno's demand that the country go back to the 1945 Constitution, the army chief of staff simply browbeat some of the Muslim delegates until he had the formality of their acceptance of the 1945 constitution, and the assembly was then told to shut up, pack up, and go home. Soekarno announced that the constitution was in force. Had the assembly consisted of men and women of great substance, debating the conditions for their support of the state, Indonesia would be another country, under rule of law. In reality, the assembly had neither money nor armed men; the army now had both, and rule of law was not to their advantage.[8]

Unfortunately for Soekarno, by seizing the country's major resources the army had stolen his clothes. They proceeded to entrench themselves deeply in the economy[9], and by reading the constitution in their own interest came to dominate the political system, so precluding any challenge to their authority. The attempt in late 1965 by a left-wing conspiracy known as *Gestapu* to challenge their position served only to show, at the cost of several hundred thousand lives, how impregnable it was. The situation has not altered; the country's major resources remain in the hands of the state, being often worked either by firms headed by the president's relatives, his associates, military formations, or foreign investors. The associates are usually of Chinese descent, and thus not part of the political public, and neither of course are the foreign investors. There is therefore nothing to compel the state to answer to its citizens; and it does not.

Not often recognized is the extent to which in Singapore, as in the pre-war Netherlands Indies, rule of law is related to the flow of resources. In a work published in 1980, a prominent author revealed that

> '... in the manufacturing sector, firms with foreign equity capital accounted in 1975 for over 65 per cent of total value-added industries, 85.3 per cent of fixed assets and 91.1 percent of direct exports. Foreign investments dominated most of the industry groups, particularly the more dynamic high value-added industries. [On the other hand] ... the Government, and not the Singapore private sector, through Temasek Holdings (formerly Ministry of Finance Incorporated), provides much of the rest of the nation's economic muscle. Temasek directly gives 24,000 people employment, with thousands more given jobs through associated companies. It has direct or boardroom control over some seventy companies in commercial, industrial and leisure fields. It controls the largest shipyard, the national airline, the third largest bank, the national shipping line, and a significant stake in the equity of nine companies quoted on the Stock Exchange. All the directors of Temasek Holdings are Government officials. ... one in every five persons employed in Singapore is paid one way or another out of public funds.'[10]

The state has not significantly relinquished its hold over the economy since. As a more recent writer points out, the Singapore government owns highly profitable enterprises such as Singapore Telecom and the Port of Singapore Authority. In addition, citizens make compulsory contributions to a Central Provident Fund. The government pays a rate of interest much lower than the market; the difference is invested in various projects, particularly housebuilding programmes, the rents on which accrue to government, and which it uses to subsidize foreign investment.[11] It also derives great political control thereby.

'About 80% of Singaporeans live in public housing provided by the Government, a situation which allows the government a very effective means of control. A person can be evicted or denied a house if they do not conform. The Housing Development Board, a government organisation responsible for the administration of this scheme, has been given the absolute power to summarily evict anyone without any redress to the courts.'[12]

The picture is plain enough. The Singapore government's principal financial support is provided either by foreign investors, or by its own firms, principally the former. It 'has become heavily dependent on capital and technology from industrialized countries... The multinationals ... have overshadowed the domestic firms...'.[13] In brief, the government for its resources depends on foreign investors; accordingly, it is only to them that rule of law applies (by way of an appeal to the Privy Council in London). For Singapore citizens there is only 'indoctrination in uncritical obedience'.[14]

In Thailand under the absolute monarchy, military and civil officials were on the one hand controlled by the king and aristocracy, and on the other united against them. The revolution of 1932 was a joint effort, but could not have succeeded without the military. With the king's powers restricted to those of a constitutional monarch, the civilians found they had been riding a tiger; '... dominance by the army is an outgrowth of the reduction of royal power'.[15]

Military power and resources have continued to increase. At the time of writing, the allocation to the Ministry of Defence amounts to between 15 and 20 per cent of the national budget.[16] The distribution and audit of this large sum are kept within the ministry, which also operates several industrial undertakings, as well as being a major shareholder in a private bank.[17]

To ensure political control, serving or retired officers form the majority in the upper house, the Senate, which has certain veto powers over legislation drawn up by the elected lower house.[18] Not content with control over the politicians, the military, specifically the army, place a substantial proportion of their forces not at the country's borders, prepared to defend them, but in the capital, ready to meet any popular challenge to their position.[19]

After their shooting of pro-democracy protesters in 1992, and consequent intervention by the king, the military promised to stay out of politics. Indeed, on 27 August, 1995 the Supreme Commander declared 'There will be no *coup d'état*'; much the same thing was said by his successor the following January.[20] These, however, are statements not of servants to their master, but of masters to their parliamentary servants. Controlling their own resources, the military remain under no rule of law, and are ready to use force whenever they consider desirable, and to legitimize their actions subsequently.

The situation in Japan is quite different, with substantial resources in the private sector, and the government dependent for its continued operation on taxes raised, with the military budget under parliamentary control, and rule of law in force.

To summarize, then, one might say that the less dependent a state is on its citizens for resources, the less likely it is to accept rule of law, and vice versa.

In the last few years of the 20th century, however, it would be misleading to limit a consideration of the checks on arbitrary government simply to internal institutions. This is particularly the case for those states discussed in this volume where judicial independence is at least questionable. For, like many other industrializing countries, they have based their development on the import of foreign capital, both public and private. It has therefore not been necessary - if indeed it had been possible - to resort to a totalitarian system of forced levies to produce resources for industrialization, as practised by the former Soviet Union and its satellites, as well as China under its late leader Mao Dzedong. By so doing they have, of course, made themselves dependent on a continuing flow of technologies, in particular innovations, which they are currently incapable of evolving themselves. The late President Soekarno of Indonesia's anguished cry in his 1964 independence day speech 'To hell with your aid!' was, in political parlance, an admission of his dependence. So also, as we have seen, is Singapore's allowing only foreigners to appeal to the Privy Council in England. The same acknowledgement may be seen in the assertions by certain Asian leaders that 'Asian values' do not permit human rights; a latter-day version of the Soepomo doctrine analysed by Buyung Nasution above, and relying on the general Western ignorance of Asian culture.[21] Such leaders are in effect acknowledging that they cannot ignore the external pressures opposing arbitrary government.

In effect, it is no longer possible for Western companies to trade with, or their governments to aid, foreign countries without questions being asked by their citizens[22] about the observance of civil and human rights by the trading partners or recipients of aid. Those countries which have suppressed the independence of their judges, who at least understood their own society and were subject to its informal controls, may find themselves constrained by the force of a less empathic Western public opinion.

References

1. Jaudel, E. (1990), p. 27.
2. Jayeratnam, J.B. (1990), p. 37.
3. The principal provisions of this document may be of interest:
    i. A declaration that the Church is free.
    ii. Feudal obligations to be defined and limited.
    iii. Law courts to be held at fixed places, assize courts to be established, and earls and barons to be tried by their peers [i.e., not by the king's men].
      iv. No extraordinary taxation without consent.
      v. No banishment or imprisonment save by judgment of peers and the law of the land.
      vi. No denial, sale, or delay of justice.
    vii. One standard of weights and measures. McKechnie, W.S. (1905).
    Nearly eight centuries later, these rights sadly remain only an aspiration for most peoples in the world.

4. The sacred nature ascribed to kingship in Medieval Europe is sometimes invoked to explain why these armed men did not simply depose the king and rule themselves, or through one of their number, as would be usual in our own day. The recorded facts suggest, however, that though Julius Caesar preferred to be king in Gaul rather than senator at Rome, in early 13th century England it was better to be baron than king. In this respect, there has been little change.

5. Zinkin, M. (1995), in *Asian Affairs*, p. 316.

6. For an account of these events see Kahin, G.M. (1952), p. 151.

7. Feith, H. (1962), p. 584.

8. In 1951, when the present writer first visited Indonesia, still to be seen on the walls of houses ruined in the fighting between Dutch and Indonesians, was the slogan (in English) 'We want a state of law'. Since then, much has been built, but the demand remains unfulfilled.

9. For details of military involvement in the economy see Crouch, H. (1978).

10. Josey, A. (1980), p. 196.

11. Davis, F. (1996) Letter in *The Times*, 5 January, p. 15.

12. Jeyaretnam, J.B. (1990), p. 32.

13. Tyabji, A. (1985), p. 31.

14. De Gucht, K. (1990), p. 57.

15. Wilson, D.A. (1962), pp. 171-174, 193.

16. *Far Eastern Economic Review* (1996), 18 January, p. 22.

17. Wilson, D.A. (1962), p. 184.

18. *Far Eastern Economic Review, ibid.*

19. Wilson, D.A. (1959), p. 37.

20. *Ibid.* (1996), 18 January, p.22

21. '... constant invocations to the "Asian" system of values are made, which include "Confucian" values ... They carefully ignore that part of Confucius which states that the people not only have the right, but also the duty, to protest against a government or authority that is unjust or evil.' Jeyaretnam, J.B. (1990), p. 38.

22. Now of course represented by a large number of groups supporting human rights, to be found in the United Nations, national parliaments, the European Parliament, and also of a private nature.

Bibliography

Amnesty International (1992), *Report 1992*, London.

Anwar, R. (ed) (1980), *Mengenang Sjahrir* [Remembering Sjahrir], Gramedia, Jakarta.

Arendt, H. (1960), *The origins of totalitarianism*, Meridian Books, New York.

Asian Cultural Forum on Development (1993), *Our voice: Bangkok NGO declaration on human rights*, Bangkok.

Bangkok Post (1992a), *Bangkok Post Year End Review 1992*, Bangkok Post, Bangkok.

Bangkok Post (1992b), *Catalyst for change: uprising in May*, Bangkok Post, Bangkok.

Barnett, D., (1967), *Cadres, Bureaucracy, and Political Power in Communist China*. Columbia U.P., New York.

Baron, B. (ed) (1991), *Philanthropy and the dynamics of change in East and Southeast Asia*. Columbia University Press, New York.

Braddell, R. St John (1982), *The Law of the Straits Settlements,* Oxford University Press, Kuala Lumpur.

Chamarik, S. (1988), *The development of human rights in Thailand*, Union of Civil Liberties, Bangkok.

Compton, B.R. (1993), *Kemelut demokrasi liberal: surat-surat rahasia Boyd R. Compton* [The crisis of liberal democracy: confidential letters by Boyd R. Compton]. LP3ES, Jakarta.

Crouch, H. (1978*), The army and poolitics in Indonesia*, Cornell University Press, Ithaca, N.Y.

Dahm, B. (1969), *Soekarno and the struggle for Indonesian independence*, (revised and updated edition of *Soekarno kampf um Indonesiens unabhangigkeit*), translated by Somers Heidhues, M.F., Cornell U.P., Ithaca, N.Y.

Dahm, B. (1987), *Sukarno: biografi politik*, LP3ES, Jakarta.

De Gucht, K. (1990), 'Statement' in Kehma-S/Grael, pp. 55-58.

Du, Xi-Chuan and Zhang, Ling-Yuan (1990), *China's legal system: a general survey*. New World Press, Beijing.

Feith, H. (1962), *The decline of constitutional democracy in Indonesia*, Cornell U.P., Ithaca, N.Y.

Finn, J.E. (1991), *Constitutions in crisis; political violence and the rule of law*, Oxford University Press, New York.

Furnivall, J.S. (1944), *Netherlands India*, University Press, Cambridge.

Japanese Government General Affairs Agency (ed) (1984), *Chusaku gyosei-tetsuduki-ho* [Commentary on the law on administrative procedures].

Greenberg, D. *et al.* (eds) (1993), *Constitutionalism and democracy: transition in the contemporary world,* Oxford University Press, New York.

Hakim, A.G.N. *et al.* (1991). *Konstitusionalisme peranan DPR dan judicial review* [Constitutionalism, role of the *DPR* and judicial review], edited by Harman B.K. & Hendardi, YLBHI & JARIM, Jakarta.

Hazairin (1973), *Demokrasi Pancasila* [Pancasila Democracy], Tintamas, Jakarta.

Hinton, H.C. (1963), 'China' in G.M. Kahin (ed), pp. 1-149.

Human Rights Watch (1993), *World Report 1993*, New York.

Ike, N. (1963), 'Japan' in Kahin, G.M. (ed), pp. 151-265.

Ilwain C.H. (1961), *Constitutionalism ancient and modern*, Cornell University Press, Ithaca, N.Y.

Jamnarnwej, W. and Muntarbhorn, V. (eds) (1992), *To human rights: rights or duties in contemporary Thailand?*, Chulalongkorn University, Bangkok.

Jaudel, Etienne (1990), 'Assessment of the state of human rights in Malaysia and Singapore from an international perspective', in Kehma-S/Grael, pp. 23-29.

Jenkin, D. (1984), *Soeharto and his generals: Indonesia military politics 1975-1983*, Modern Indonesia Project Monograph No. 64, Cornell University, Ithaca, N.Y.

Jeyaretnam, J.B. (1990), 'The rule of law in Singapore' in Kehma-S/Grael, pp. 30-38.

Johnson, C. (1982), *MITI and the Japanese miracle*, Charles Tuttle, Tokyo.

Josey, A. (1980), *Singapore, its past, present, and future*, André Deutsch, London.

Kahin, G. McT. (1952), *Nationalism and revolution in Indonesia,* Cornell University Press, Ithaca, N.Y.

Kahin, G.M. (ed) (1959), *Governments and politics of Southeast Asia,* Cornell University Press, Ithaca, N.Y.

Kahin, G.M. (ed) (1963), *Major Governments of Asia*, Cornell University Press, Ithaca, N.Y.

Kehma-S/Grael (1990), *The rule of law and human rights in Malaysia and Singapore: a report of the conference held at the European Parliament, Brussels, 9 & 10 March 1989.* Organised by Kehma-S (The European Committee for Human Rights in Malaysia and Singapore) and the GRAEL in the Rainbow Group, European Parliament. Forum, Selangor.

Koesnodiprodjo (1951), *Himpunan undang-undang, peraturan-peraturan, penetapan-penetapan Pemerintah Republik Indonesia 1945.* [Compilation of government laws, regulations, and decrees of the Government of the Republic of Indonesia 1945]), S. K. Seno, Jakarta.

Kosananand, C. (1985), *Law, rights and liberties in Thai society*, Coordinating Committee for Religion in Society, Bangkok.

Kraivichien, T. (1967), *The administration of justice in Thailand*, Thai Bar Association, Bangkok.

Legge, J.D. (1972), *Soekarno: a political biography*, Allen Lane The Penguin Press, London.

Lev, D.S. (1966). *The Transition to Guided Democracy: Indonesian Politics, 1957-1959*, Cornell Modern Indonesia Project, Ithaca, N.Y.

Lev, D.S. (1990), *'Gerakan sosial, konstitusionalisme dan hak asasi'* ['Social movements, constitutionalism, and human rights'] in *Hukum dan politik di Indonesia: kesinumbungan dan perubahan* [Law and politics in Indonesia: continuity and change], LP3ES, Jakarta, pp. 514-515.

Lubis, T.M. (1993), *In search of human rights*, Gramedia/SPES, Jakarta.

Mahakun, V. (1992), *The fight for judicial independence*, Group for the Protection of the Judiciary, Bangkok (in Thai).

Malaka, T. (1948), *Dari pendjara ke pendjara* [From prison to prison], vol. 2, stencilled, privately published.

Malik, Y.K. and V.B. Singh (1994), *Hindu nationalists in India: the rise of the Bharatiya Janata Party*, Westview Press, Boulder, Col., and Oxford.

Matsushita, M. (1993), *International trade and competition law in Japan*, Oxford University Press, Oxford.

McKechnie, W.S. (1905), *Magna Carta*, Maclehose, Glasgow.

MITI (ed) (1992), *Final report of the SII talks*, MITI, Tokyo.

Morell, D. and Samudvanija, C. (1982*), Political conflict in Thailand: reform, reaction and revolution*, Oelgeschlager, Gunn & Hain, Cambridge, Mass.

Muntarbhorn, V. (1992), *Towards a Thai legal system: from delivery to deliverance?* Paper presented at the Asian Law Conference, Chiangmai, 31 August-4 September.

Nanakorn, K. (1992), *The criminal process in Thailand: identification of problems and recommendations for reform,* paper presented at the Asian Law Conference, Chiangmai, 31 August - 4 September.

Nasution, A.B. (1993a), *The aspiration for constitutional government in Indonesia: a socio-legal study of the Indonesian* Konstituante *1956-1959*, Utrecht: Utrecht University; (1993), Jakarta, Sinar Harapan.

Nasution, A.B. (1993b) *'Staatsidee integralistik dan sistem ketatanegaraan Indonesia'* [The idea of the integral state and the Indonesian form of government], paper presented at a seminar held at Gadjah Mada University, Yogyakarta.

Nasution, A.H. (1981), *Inti konsensus nasional 1966: laksanakan UUD '45 secara murni & konsequen* [The core of the national consensus of 1966: implement the 1945 constitution in a genuine and responsible manner]. Yayasan Lembaga Kesadaran Berkonstitusi, Jakarta.

Nasution, A.H. (1984). *Memenuhi panggilan tugas* [Responding to the call of duty], Gunung Agung, Jakarta, vol. 4.

Nikkei (ed) (1980), *Daiten-ho ga Kieru toki* [When the law on large scale shops disappears], Nikkei, Tokyo.

Noer, D. (1987). *Partai Islam di pentas nasional 1945-1965* [Islamic parties on the national stage 1945-1965], Grafitipers, Jakarta.

Notosusanto, N. (ed) (1985), *Tercapainya konsensus nasional* [Achievement of national consensus 1966-1969] *1966-1969*, Balai Pustaka, Jakarta.

Oda, H. (1992), *Japanese Law*, Butterworths, London.

Oda, H. (ed) (1994), *Japanese commercial law in the era of internationalization*, Graham & Trottman, London.

O'Donnell, G., Schmitter, P.C. & Whitehead, L. (eds) (1986), *Transitions from authoritarian rule: southern Europe. Transitions from authoritarian rule: comparative perspectives. Transitions from authoritarian rule: tentative conclusions about uncertain democracies.* Johns Hopkins University Press, Baltimore.

Parlour, R. (ed) (1994), *Encyclopedia of laws against money laundering*, Butterworths, London.

Pe, C. *et al.* (eds), (1988) *Transcultural mediation in Asia-Pacific*, Asia-Pacific Organization for Mediation, Manila.

Peters, A.A.G. & Koesriani, S. (1990), *Hukum dan perkembangan sosial* [Law and social development], Sinar Harapan, Jakarta, vol. 3.

Physicians for Human Rights and Asiawatch (1992), *Thailand: bloody May - excessive use of lethal force in Bangkok*, Boston/New York.

Poompanna, A. (1991), *Insight into Santi Asoke II*. Dharma Santi Foundation, Bangkok.

Pringgodigdo, A.K. (n.d.), *Perubahan kabinet presidentiil menjadi kabinet parlementer* [Changing a presidential cabinet to a parliamentary cabinet], Yayasan Fond, Universitit Gajah Mada.

Purwokusumo, S. (1951), *Pemberontakan Madiun ditinjau dari hukum negara kita* [The Madiun rebellion considered in the light of the laws of our state], Sumber Kemajuan Rakyat, Jogyakarta.

Quah, J.S.T., *et al.* (eds) (1985), *Government and politics of Singapore.* Oxford University Press, Singapore.

Redden and Schlueter (eds) (1990), *Modern legal systems cyclopedia*, vol. 9A Asia, Hein & Co., New York.

Regional Council on Human Rights in Asia (1980), *The law and practice of preventive detention in the ASEAN region*, Manila.

Ricklefs, M.C. (1991), *Sejarah Indonesia modern* [A history of modern Indonesia]. Gadjah Mada University Press, Jogyakarta.

Robinson, R. (1984), *Sejarah politik Orde Baru* [A political history of the New Order], Lembaga Studi Pembangunan, Jakarta.

Seputra, P. (1973) *Beberapa aspek dari sejarah Indonesia* [Various aspects of Indonesian history], Nusa Indah, Ende, Flores.

Shiono, H. (1994), *Gyosei-ho* [Administrative law], part I, 2nd ed, Yuhikaku, Tokyo.

Shintou, M. (1992), *Gyosei-shido* [Administrative guidance], Iwanami, Tokyo.

Simorangkir, J.C.T., and Say, B.M.R. (1975), *Konstitusi dan Konstituante* [Constitution and Constituent Assembly], Yayasan Komunikasi, Jakarta

Sjahrir (1990), *Renungan dan perjuangan* [Reflections and struggles], Dian Rakyat, Jakarta.

Simanjuntak, M. (1994), *Pandangan negara integralistik* [Philosophy of the integral state], Grafiti Pers, Jakarta.

Snouck Hurgronje, C. (1906), *The Achehnese*, Vol. 1, E.J. Brill, Leyden.

Sobhakvichitr, K. (1980), *The protection of human rights in Thai law*, Chulalongkorn University, Bangkok.

Soedjono, R. (1993), *Demokratisasi dan integrasi nasional dalam konteks globalisasi: perspektif sospol ABRI* [Democracy and national integration in the context of globalisation: the socio-political perspective of the armed forces]. Paper given at a seminar on 21 September of CESDA-LP3ES, Jakarta.

Soekarno (1961), *Resopim: revolusi-sosialisme Indonesia-pimpinan nasional* [Resopim: revolution - Indonesian socialism - national leadership], Departemen Penerangan [Department of Information], Jakarta.

Tshisungu, J. (ed) (1992), *The media and the human rights challenge*, Canadian Human Rights Foundation, Montreal.

Tuji, K. (ed) (1984), *Public Administration in Japan*, University of Tokyo Press, Tokyo.

Tyabji, A. (1985), 'The economy' in Quah, J.S.T. *et al.* (eds), pp. 25-44.

United Nations Development Programme (1993), *Human Development Report 1993*, Oxford University Press, Oxford.

Vella, W. (1957), *Siam under Rama III 1824-1851*, J.J. Augustin, New York.

Wilson, D.A. (1959), 'Thailand' in Kahin, G.M., pp. 3-72.

Wilson, D.A. (1962), *Politics in Thailand*. Cornell University Press, Ithaca, N.Y.

Wright, J. (1991), *The balancing act: a history of modern Thailand*, Asia Books, Bangkok.

Yamin, M. (1959), *Naskah Persiapan Undang-Undang Dasar 1945* [Draft of the 1945 Constitution]. Penerbit Prapantja, Jakarta, vol. 1.

Zheng, H. (1988), *China's Civil and Commercial Law*, Butterworths, London.

Zinkin, M., (1995), in *Asian Affairs*, XXXVI, III, Oct., pp. 314-317 (review of Malik, Y.K. and V.B. Singh (1994).